"It may surprise you to learn that I did not want to write this book. Moreover, I hope the premise and everything I forecast turn out to be dead wrong. Everyone, including me, will be much better off if that is true. The problem is that all the evidence shows I am right."

—Stephen Leeb

Acclaim for Author Stephen Leeb's Previous Books

"A blockbuster. A powerful warning coupled with well-documented advice."

—Myron Kandel, former editor and anchor,
CNN Financial News

"Brilliantly and superbly written. Truly impressive . . . Cannily guides investors faced with the prospect of an alarming, all-too-likely scenario."

—Gene G. Marcial, senior writer
and "Inside Wall Street" columnist, *BusinessWeek*

"Leeb spins advice that can survive the siege."

—*U.S. News and World Report*

"Brazen, brilliant . . . and a little bit frightening. Provocative and prophetic, this is one of the most important books I've read in years. Those who heed its strategies will be richly rewarded."

—Jonathan Hoenig, portfolio manager,
Capitalistpig Hedge Fund, LLC, and author of *Greed Is Good*

The Coming Economic Collapse

How You Can Thrive When Oil Costs $200 a Barrel

Stephen Leeb, PhD,
with **Glen C. Strathy**

BUSINESS PLUS

NEW YORK   BOSTON

Business Plus
Hachette Book Group USA
237 Park Avenue
New York, NY 10017

Visit our Web site at www.HachetteBookGroupUSA.com.

Printed in the United States of America

Originally published in hardcover by Hachette Book Group USA.

First Trade Edition: February 2007

10 9 8 7 6 5 4 3

Business Plus is an imprint of Grand Central Publishing.
The Business Plus name and logo is a trademark of Hachette Book Group USA, Inc.

Library of Congress Cataloging-in-Publication Data
Leeb, Stephen
   The coming economic collapse : how you can thrive when oil costs $200 a barrel / Stephen Leeb, with Glen Strathy.— 1st ed.
      p. cm.
   Includes bibliographical references.
   ISBN-13: 978-0446-57978-0
   ISBN-10: 0-446-57978-5
   1. Economic forecasting—United States. 2. Petroleum products—Prices. 3. Nonrenewable natural resources. 4. Energy consumption. 5. Investments. I. Strathy, Glen. II. Title.
   HC106.83.I44 2006
   330.9001'12—dc22

                                                                        2005033288

ISBN 978-0-446-69900-6 (pbk.)

Acknowledgments

The authors extend their special thanks to
Genia Turanova and the folks at *The Complete Investor*,
who aided this project, as well as to Donna Leeb,
Kaitlin Rainey, and Jillian Strathy, whose support,
patience, and advice made it possible.

Contents

Author's Note

I t may surprise you to learn that I did not want to write this book. Moreover, I hope the premise and everything I forecast turn out to be dead wrong. Everyone including me will be much better off if that is true. The problem is that all the evidence shows I am right.

In early 2004, I published a book called *The Oil Factor*, which I intended to be an investment guide for the next few years. It was clear to me at the time that analysts had severely underestimated future demand for oil and overestimated potential supply. I felt this growing mismatch between supply and demand for oil, and natural gas as well, would lead to much higher energy prices.

Though I recommended a few alternative energy stocks, I wasn't trying to proselytize for alternative energies. After all, *The Oil Factor* was primarily an investment book. I hoped readers would find the ideas valuable and make some money in oil while the rest of the world took action on the energy problem. I had an abiding faith that the markets and government would react appropriately once the crisis was recognized. In other words, it seemed clear all we needed was a wake-up call and either industry or, more likely, a consortium of industry and government would embark on a crash program to develop wind and other alternative energies.

In the two years since then, energy as I expected has performed extremely well. My prediction of oil at $100 a barrel, which many found so outlandish in 2004, now seems well within reach. So why shouldn't I just take a bow and quit?

Because I have realized the oil situation is much more important than an investment theme. It is evolving into a civilization-threatening crisis. What made this clear to me was the one question I had the most trouble answering during interviews and discussions about *The Oil Factor*: "Why are you the only one—or at best one of a very small minority—who sees the oil crisis unfolding? After all, if it really is a crisis wouldn't everyone be aware of it?"

Was it possible that only a few of us saw that today's popular beliefs regarding oil were false, that in fact the emperor had no clothes? Was it possible that all those whom I had talked with—including Harvard professors, Wall Street analysts, government opinion makers, and oil company executives—were missing something so obvious?

Two books convinced me that our civilization was falling prey to colossal errors of judgment: *Collapse*, by Jared Diamond, and *The Collapse of Complex Societies*, by Joseph Tainter. These books graphically delineate how many past civilizations fell because their leaders did not prepare for a shortage of resources.

After reading these books, I realized that the fault did not lie in the peculiarities of the individual civilization but rather were grounded in universal human characteristics—characteristics revealed by the well-known Milgram and Asch experiments that we briefly describe in chapter 4. You don't have to have a PhD in psychology (and I do) to realize that what happened to past civilizations could easily happen to us.

If I felt it was already too late to solve the energy problem, I would not have bothered writing this book. Make no mistake, the situation is dire. If you were one of the millions of investors caught in the bursting of the technology bubble in 2000, you should know that the coming energy crisis will be far more damaging.

However, as you will learn, the crisis can be avoided. Even though time is very short, solutions exist that can help us wean ourselves off our dependency on oil.

I am hopeful we will take the right steps in time, because I know that Americans, when faced with a crisis, excel at rolling up their sleeves and putting things right. But first we have to realize the problem exists.

Within our human tendency to defer to others lie the seeds of our own undoing. Our salvation must come from being willing to trust in and think for ourselves. This book is my best attempt to convince you.

Stephen Leeb, PhD

The Bursting of the Tech Bubble: Did Our Most Recent Brush with Disaster Teach Us Anything?

An economic crisis is near at hand in America today, the kind of dramatic, earth-shattering crisis that periodically threatens the very survival of civilization. More specifically, it is an energy crisis brought about by the conflict between rising global demand for energy and our growing inability to increase energy production.

I first drew attention to this crisis in my 2004 book, *The Oil Factor*. The book was controversial, particularly because of its prediction that oil prices would reach $100 a barrel by the end of this decade. Since its publication, oil, gasoline, and natural gas prices have hit historic highs. Meanwhile, energy supply/demand fundamentals have worsened to the point that it now appears $200 a barrel by the end of the decade is entirely probable. Naturally, the negative impact this will have on our economy, not to mention your pocketbook, will be considerable.

However, what alarms us most about this crisis is the extent to which our nation's leaders and experts remain in denial concerning it. Most authorities continue to reassure the public that today's soaring energy prices are temporary, that oil reserves are virtually limitless, and that production will outpace demand for the remainder of our lives. This is an outright contradiction of the facts. The trends in place for the last thirty years show declining returns from oil exploration, peaking or declining oil production everywhere but in a few OPEC nations, and increasing demand for energy, especially among the world's largest developing nations.

You may find it hard to believe the experts could be so wrong. Naturally, most of us are inclined to trust in the wisdom and honesty of our leaders. We ourselves are horrified that so few are raising the alarm. Why is such a serious threat not on the front pages of every newspaper? Why are government and industry not taking steps right now to prevent the crisis?

Unfortunately, this is not the first time in recent years that a major economic threat has gone unacknowledged by our leaders. In the most significant example, until the moment when the ax fell, everyone, including corporate executives, Wall Street analysts, and the media, portrayed the situation in glowingly optimistic terms. Rather than try to prevent a crisis, most authorities actually encouraged people to act in a way that brought them greater financial loss and made the economic impact worse. We are speaking of the rise and fall of the technology bubble.

In that brush with disaster, which came much closer to destroying our economy than most people realize, we see a mirror image of what is happening today with energy. If we are to weather the energy crisis successfully, both as investors and as a society, we need to understand why similar errors in judgment are occurring, and what we must do to correct them in time.

The Madness of the Herd

It is no exaggeration to say that in the late 1990s the investment world went mad. Millions upon millions of investors ignored time-honored principles for investing in stocks, such as due diligence and fundamental analysis, and began to buy and sell purely out of emotion. Believing in the wonders of technology, they rushed to buy technology and Internet stocks like rats following a Wall Street pied piper.

The result was a financial and economic crisis that destroyed the financial security of millions of investors. However, what few people realize is how close the technology crash came to destroying our economy and even our society as a whole.

I recall one client who phoned me near the height of the bubble, in 1999. I knew him personally. We had been managing his portfolio for some time, and it had been doing quite well by typical investment standards—gaining roughly 20 percent annually.

But on this day, he announced that he wanted to handle his own investments from then on. When I asked him why, he said he wanted more technology shares in his portfolio. Clearly, he had been bitten by the high-tech mania that was spreading through the markets at the time.

Of course, there is nothing wrong with someone making his own investment decisions. However, as a professional money manager, I can tell you that it is not an easy job, especially if you are trying to make returns that are well above average. Anyone can get lucky enough to beat the market for a short time. But most of the people who do so find their luck lasts only a brief while. To beat the long-term returns of the market, without taking on excessive risk of loss, and to do so consistently, is extremely difficult.

Like many firms, we have a full-time staff that studies the markets and the economies around the world, applying detailed analytic methods, in order to stay on top of trends and spot opportunities. The result is that our model portfolios have been able to outperform the market—which means outperforming not only the average investor, but also the average professional— much of the time. However, that is the result of in-depth knowledge, long hours of hard work, and a good deal of experience. It would be nearly impossible for someone with a full-time job to duplicate single-handedly the work we do.

Now, this man had a full-time job. He owned his own business. While he was highly educated and intelligent, he did not have time to gain more than a superficial knowledge of stocks. Instead, his method of managing his portfolio was literally to run over to a television set between clients and turn on CNBC to get the latest tech tip, which he would then follow. Over the next few months, he sold every stock in his portfolio that was not technology-related, and put all his retirement savings into tech stocks. Many of his new holdings were companies he knew nothing about. He just saw them on television.

I am certain you can guess the result. In a period of about nine to twelve months, this man lost roughly 70 percent of his retirement savings.

It is nearly impossible for an investor to recover from a loss like this. A 70 percent loss on, for instance, a $100,000 portfolio leaves its owner with only $30,000. Even if the owner manages to double his money before retirement, that still leaves him with $40,000 less than he had at the peak.

And this man's case was far from unusual. I knew many bright, well-educated people during that period who were convinced that "this time it is different"—that the tech bubble was not a false mania, like the South Sea Bubble or the late 1920s. It was the real thing. A new paradigm had taken hold. A new world was dawning in which a company's present earnings, assets, and debt levels did not matter. As long as a company had innovative technology, or could sell products from a Web site, its stock was sure to make investors rich. Hordes of people believed they could not go wrong buying tech stocks, and feared nothing except missing the opportunity. Many risked more money than they had by buying stocks on margin or with other forms of borrowed cash.

What the majority of investors had forgotten, or perhaps never stopped to think about, was that the victims of past speculative manias had been just as certain of becoming rich.

But that is the nature of speculative manias: people en masse forsake reason and objective thinking and succumb to a primordial instinct to run with the herd. Hundreds of years ago, when a herd of buffalo was stampeded toward a cliff by Native American hunters, no buffalo poked his head above the crowd to look where they were going. Each creature simply accepted his neighbors' belief that there was an urgent need to run. From then on, they were driven by pure adrenaline, each buffalo's panic and excitement reinforcing his neighbors'. So it was with investors in the tech bubble. Greed, and a fear of being left behind, triggered the same instinctive state of excitement and panic that kept everyone's eyes glued to the financial media, their fingers hovering over the trigger buttons of their stock trading programs.

When the bubble burst, the result was financial suffering and loss on a scale bigger than anything since the Great Depression. The NASDAQ fell from 5,000 points to just over 1,000. Many of the technology and Internet companies to which average people had hitched their future went bankrupt, or were forced to downsize. We were left with a massively overbuilt tech industry and a much poorer consumer. Trillions of dollars of wealth were lost that could have financed the retirement plans, the college funds, and the other hopes and dreams of millions of investors.

Even worse, the popping of the technology bubble put the U.S. economy in an extremely perilous situation. The very fabric of our civilization came close to disintegrating.

What saved us from disaster was the rapid response from our leaders. The Federal Reserve stabilized our economy by quickly lowering interest rates to nearly zero, and in real terms to less than zero. The federal government cut taxes aggressively. Manufacturers offered zero percent financing on cars—actually less than zero, when you subtract inflation. Consumers were virtually spoon-fed money.

Low interest rates also provided a free lunch for those who refinanced their mortgages. In effect, the surge in home refinancing and the perception that home values would rise faster than mortgage rates gave the consumer a double boost. More money became available to spend, and the value of homes increased.

Without that quick response, the results could have been catastrophic. Consumers would have had far less money to spend. With the resulting decline in consumer spending, it would be hard to exaggerate how severe the recession might have become.

Remarkably, in the wake of September 11, 2001, Americans still kept their faith in the future. Yet that faith could have been shaken to the core if the number of jobs started to dry up, if home values began to fall, and if consumers suddenly found themselves without the means to pay off their huge debt loads.

Clearly, there would have been a drastic change in the consumer psyche. Fear would have replaced faith. Income levels could have fallen so far that future tax cuts would have had little positive effect (there would have been much less income on which to cut taxes). The same would have been true for cuts in interest rates. If the Fed had waited until after home prices had started falling to lower interest rates, the huge financial windfall that came from home refinancing would never have occurred.

Economic weakness would have led to increased consumer fears, which in turn would have led to greater weakness. The banks, which hold the debt of our highly leveraged society, could have been severely stressed. New lending would have been curtailed, and no doubt all but the strongest banks would have been tottering. It would have been a vicious circle of consumer fears, less spending, weakening banks, falling home and asset prices, ever greater consumer fears, further declines in spending, threats to even the strongest banks, and crashing home and stock values. Once this vicious circle took hold it would have been extremely difficult, if not impossible, to save the economy.

Fortunately, our leaders did the right thing. The unprecedented amount of liquidity rescued our economy, and society as a whole. The collapse of many tech companies led to less capacity. Stocks began to rally. Eventually, the all-too-real threat of a vicious circle became something of a virtuous circle.

All in all, we were very lucky to survive the tech bubble. We were lucky to handle the aftermath in a short space of time. We were lucky we had the ability to flood the economy with liquidity so quickly. The crisis we face today in oil cannot be solved as easily. We may not be so fortunate this time.

The Inescapable Truth About Technology

As individual investors, there is little we can do to prevent mass hysteria from occurring, let alone the imbalances in society that can provoke a major economic crisis such as the tech bubble or the growing oil squeeze. We can, however, learn to avoid such ill-founded hysteria ourselves. Moreover, as the energy crisis unfolds, we must acquire the ability to protect ourselves financially, and grow wealthier, despite the resulting turmoil.

The most important question raised by the technology crash is why so many intelligent people—professionals and nonprofessionals alike—did not see the bubble for what it was. What fooled them into pursuing such a mad course of action that inflicted so much damage to their own future?

Because, of course, it was a kind of madness. It was a madness based on the false belief that technological progress would continue to rise exponentially, solve all of the world's problems, and make every investor a multimillionaire within a few short years.

In reality, technology could do none of those things. In my 1999 book, *Defying the Market*, I pointed out that, contrary to popular belief, the rate of technological progress has begun to decline. For example, in the early part of the twentieth century, science made major breakthroughs at a rate of five or more per decade. However, since the 1960s, the rate of breakthroughs has decreased. There were only three in the 1970s (quantum cosmology, chaos theory and fractals, and antiviral drugs), one in the 1980s (DNA replication), and none since.

Improvements in computer technology have also slowed, with the latest generation of computer chips only slightly faster than their predecessors, and the most popular software packages little changed from five years ago. There have been no big medical discoveries since antiviral drugs in 1978. And in recent years, high tech has not helped us increase the world's supply of food or freshwater, or solved our pressing need for new energy sources.

The slowdown in technology follows the general pattern of human progress. Every time civilization undertakes a new profitable endeavor, the biggest gains are made in the beginning. There is no mystery to this. We naturally pursue the biggest and easiest gains first, just as, when we pick apples from a tree, we start with the best apples that are easiest to reach. Eventually, when these run out, we turn to the smaller, harder-to-reach fruit. Consequently, every endeavor—from agriculture to technology to oil production—eventually must suffer diminishing returns.

One reason for the slower pace in electronics and computer development is that we are reaching certain physical limits, such as bus speeds, and the wavelength of light used to etch silicon chips. As a result, it is increasingly difficult and expensive to make even minor gains.

It was obvious in the late 1990s that the technology industry was maturing and that the best technology stocks were not the ones developing new technology. They were companies like Dell that were making money through sound management and excellent marketing strategies to achieve a dominant position.

Yet for some reason, people's expectations for technology seemed to balloon just as the industry began to peak. Only in 2000 did investors realize the high-tech industry was not living up to their exaggerated expectations. The massive demand, sales, and profits that had been projected failed to materialize.

Of course, I was not the only person who predicted the technology bubble would end in disappointment. Others expressed similar concerns. Warren Buffett, arguably the world's most successful investor, stayed away from high-tech companies altogether.

And of course, the truth about the technology industry was available to anyone who took the time to study the matter deeply. But those of us who contradicted the herd were decried by the so-called experts at the time as over the hill, our voices drowned out by the enthusiastic ravings of the other side.

The Ubiquitous Lies

Clearly, much of what the experts said about technology stocks was inaccurate. However, while it might be tempting to create a conspiracy theory to account for what happened, the falsehoods were so widespread that it is impossible to blame a deliberate effort by any one group.

On the one hand, journalism and the media have a traditional obligation to provide accurate and unbiased reporting. For that reason, most people are inclined to trust what they see on television and in the newspapers. During the tech bubble, however, the media appeared to abandon their integrity, as they presented endlessly bullish reports that seemed expressly intended to encourage people to buy stocks. CNBC, for instance, had a birthday cake every time the NASDAQ index went up another thousand points. Thomas Friedman, the well-respected *New York Times* columnist, unquestioningly accepted the claim by John Chambers, CEO of Cisco Systems, that Cisco would be front and center in solving the country's educational problems.

George Gilder, a would-be prophet for the new religion of technology, predicted that Internet traffic would "soar a thousandfold every three to five years, more than a millionfold in a decade."[1] Certainly, Internet use will increase as computers spread throughout the developing world. But Gilder makes no mention of the fact that Internet expansion will eventually run into some very fixed limits—such as the number of people in the world, the availability of resources, and the amount of time the average person will want to spend online.

However, the media were not solely to blame. Wall Street analysts are supposed to make objective assessments of companies for the aid of investors. Yet they abandoned their objectivity as well. Analysts presented an unending stream of bullish forecasts to the public through television appearances, newspaper interviews, and other media. For major technology stocks, growth rates of 30 percent or more were considered sustainable, even though they defied rational analysis. And Wall Street continued issuing bullish forecasts right up until the bubble popped.

For instance, as late as July 2000, many Wall Street firms still rated Nortel Networks a "strong buy." Canadian Imperial Bank of Commerce (CIBC) estimated Nortel's earnings would grow by 30–35 percent in 2001, and that its stock would reach $110 a share. In the months that followed, as many investors know painfully well, Nortel shares went into free fall. Today, they trade at just over $3.

In September 2000, Salomon Smith Barney raised its target price on shares in Juniper Networks to $310. Less than a year later, they were trading at $25, and they have not budged much since.

There were predictions that Cisco, then a company with about $12 billion in revenues, would reach a market capitalization of a trillion dollars, and that it could support a price/earnings ratio of 105 (at present, its P/E ratio is just over 20, and its share price has fallen from $70 to less than $18).

Our favorite was a projection that Qualcomm stock would

---

1. George Gilder, "Build It and They Will Come," *American Spectator*, November 1, 2000.

reach $1,000. For that to happen, the company would have to sell more cell phones—indeed, many more cell phones—each year by the beginning of the next decade than there were men, women, and children on the planet. It was an outrageous prediction, and even more outrageous was that investors bought it hook, line, and sinker.

Even more astonishing, if technology had inspired mass delusion and religious fervor among Wall Street analysts and the media, the executives who ran technology companies—who had firsthand knowledge of the industry—were as unrealistically bullish as the rest. As a result, massive amounts of capital expenditure went into everything from telephone lines to fabrication plants to server farms. Underlying these enormous building programs was the undying belief that demand for tech would grow by 30 percent a year for an indefinite period.

Over ten years, a compound growth rate of 30 percent would have meant the technology industry would experience a nearly fourteen-fold gain. It implied the NASDAQ would reach a level of 70,000. Exciting, if it were true. But certainly not realistic.

Of course, there was some degree of outright dishonesty. With so much money pouring into technology and the stock market in general, the temptations for morally indifferent people in positions of power were too great to resist. A prime example of such corruption is the Enron debacle, which epitomized the false promises that were rampant.

In the tech bubble, most so-called experts bought into the delusion that technology stocks would soar to unprecedented heights. That attitude nearly destroyed the economy. Today, an equally false attitude states that oil prices will stay perpetually low. Just as, in the tech bubble, the experts kept reinforcing the delusion even as stock prices were falling, so today, as energy prices are hitting new highs, experts continue to reiterate the false claim that prices will soon return to "normal" (meaning the low level that prevailed in the 1990s).

The oil delusion is a mirror image of the technology delusion. While almost everyone in 1999 believed the bull market in technology would endure, almost everyone today believes the bull market in oil is temporary. Yet the consequence of today's delusion may be a far greater disaster than the tech crash. For, as we will see, history is littered with the ashes of societies that refused to cope with similar shortfalls in vital resources. If we wish to avoid their fate, we must understand what causes both crises and the preceding climate of denial. As both investors and citizens, we must resist herd mentality, face the growing energy crisis squarely, and form a plan to deal with it in time.

CHAPTER 2

A Collision Course
with Disaster

I n my 2004 book, *The Oil Factor*, I warned investors that an energy shortfall is brewing that could easily be the worst economic crisis our nation has ever faced. In issuing that prediction, I made no claim to be a geologist or petroleum expert. I was merely playing the role of an extrapolator, basing my conclusions on readily available published data. My purpose was to identify the most likely economic scenario for the coming decade, and prepare investors to succeed financially.

In particular, I had three points I wanted to impress on my readers. These were:

1. Since 1973 and the founding of OPEC, the price of oil has been the most important leading indicator of both the U.S. economy and the stock market.

We began with the observation that, between 1973 and 2000, our economy suffered five recessions that alternated with periods of strong growth. We also had several bear markets in stocks. When we examined the relationship between oil prices and these zigs and zags, we discovered that economic downturns and bear markets were always preceded by rising oil prices. In particular, whenever the price of oil doubled over a twelve-month period, stock returns ranged from –27 percent to +4 percent over the following eighteen months. On the other hand, if oil prices declined over a twelve-month period, stocks returned anywhere from –1 percent to +30 percent.

Taking a practical example, let us compare two hypothetical investors, each of whom put $20,000 into the S&P 500 index stocks in 1973. The first investor simply holds his stocks until 2000. The second investor sells his stocks for cash every time the year-over-year increase in oil prices is more than 80 percent (which typically signals the start of a deflationary period). He or she then reinvests in stocks when the year-over-year increase in oil falls below 20 percent (indicating a switch to inflation). By 2000, the buy-and-hold investor's portfolio would have been worth roughly thirty-five times more, or $700,000. However, the investor who followed the oil-price signals would have multiplied his capital seventy-fold, for a total of $1.4 million.

In later chapters we will provide more detailed information on how to invest profitably during the next decade. The key point to remember is that fast-rising oil prices have a major negative impact on investment returns and the strength of the economy.

2. Over the past thirty years or so, the United States has been losing control of its energy supply, and as a result our economy has grown increasingly vulnerable to external political and economic factors.

Before 1973, when the United States produced most of the oil it consumed, the relationship between economic growth and inflation followed a clear pattern. A period of strong growth would lead to rising inflation. The government would then intervene by raising interest rates and tightening the money supply. This would slow growth and cause inflation to fall. Finally, the government would lower interest rates again to stimulate growth. However, in the 1970s a major change occurred that caused this pattern to break down. The change relates to something known as "Hubbert's law."

In the 1950s, the geologist M. King Hubbert observed that once you extract half the oil from a given field, production begins to decline. Applying this law to the United States as a whole, Hubbert concluded that oil production in the United States would peak in the early 1970s.

Hubbert's conclusion proved to be correct. In 1970, U.S. production reached its all-time maximum at a little over 9 million barrels a day and has been on a slow decline ever since. Today, the nation produces roughly 5.5 million barrels a day. Coincidentally, the early 1970s also marked the first time that the United States began consuming more imported oil than domestically produced oil. Foreign oil has comprised an ever larger percentage of the oil we use ever since.

In 1973, America's new vulnerability was exposed when OPEC nations imposed restrictions on oil exports, causing a 70 percent rise in global oil prices. Shortly after, OPEC forced oil prices even higher by imposing a total embargo on oil exports. It did this to protest U.S. support for Israel in the Yom Kippur War. The spike in oil prices put a heavy strain on the American economy, resulting in a new type of malaise, dubbed "stagflation," in which growth stagnated and inflation rose at the same time.

Stagflation put the government in a bind. Should it raise interest rates to fight inflation, or lower rates to restore growth? Obviously, it could not do both, so the 1970s became the most difficult economic period since the 1930s, for average citizens and policymakers alike.

Eventually the political situation in the Middle East calmed down and oil prices fell, thanks in part to increased oil production among non-OPEC nations. Many of these nations, such as the United Kingdom and Europe, are close allies of the United States. Then, in 1999, another serious change occurred in the oil arena.

Oil production by non-OPEC nations appeared to reach its maximum level—and may in fact have begun to decline.

Now, this is a serious problem. If the United States wants continued economic growth, that growth will require additional energy. If oil is to be the source of that energy (as almost everyone assumes), what country can we rely on to supply it? Having little hope of more oil from our Western allies, we must turn to our Eastern neighbors—our Middle Eastern neighbors, to be precise.

Of course, the most important oil-producing nation is Saudi Arabia. However, we cannot be sure the Saudis will provide us with all the oil we want. In the first place, no one is entirely certain how much oil Saudi Arabia has left. Two geologists, Colin Campbell and Jean Laherrere, published an article in *Scientific American* in 1998 suggesting that the official reserve estimates for Saudi Arabia, as well as Iraq and Iran, are highly suspect and may be overstated. Matthew Simmons, author of *Twilight in the Desert*, argues that the Saudis' total proven oil reserves in 1979 were 110 billion barrels. Since then, the Saudis have extracted some 60 billion barrels—more than half. In other words, Saudi Arabian production may have already reached its peak.

In addition, the political situation in the Middle East poses another problem. The House of Saud may regard the United States as its ally, but it has to walk a fine line between Saudi Arabia's Westernized elite and the powerful religious establishment, which practices the Wahhabi form of Sunni Islam. Many of the more radical clerics in that country are decidedly anti-American.

Michael Scott Doran published an excellent analysis of the political situation in Saudi Arabia in *Foreign Affairs* (January–February 2004). He writes, "For the most radical Saudi clerics . . . enemies include Christians, Jews, Shiites, and even insufficiently devout Sunni Muslims. From the perspective of *Tawhid*, these groups constitute a grand conspiracy to destroy true Islam. The United States, the 'Idol of the Age,' leads the cabal. It attacked Sunni Muslims in

Afghanistan and Iraq, both times making common cause with Shi-ites; it supports the Jews against the Sunni Muslim Palestinians; it promotes Shiite interests in Iraq; and it presses the Saudi govern-ment to de-Wahhabize its educational curriculum."

On the flip side, Doran notes that the United States has many enemies among Shiite Muslims as well, many of whom are also suffering from the continuing unrest in Iraq: "If Washington maintains business as usual with Riyadh, it will not be long before the Iraqi Shiites will conclude that the United States covertly sup-ports the Wahhabi bombers who blow up their mosques—just as they concluded, after the events of 1991, that the United States sup-ported Saddam Hussein against them." Of course, American rela-tions with Iran, a largely Shiite country, are already less than cordial.

So it seems that the only countries that might be able to supply the United States with additional oil are the very ones whose pop-ulations exhibit the strongest anti-American sentiments in the world. Who else can we turn to if relations between these coun-tries and us sour? Venezuela? Nigeria? The former Soviet Union? Even if they could increase production, they are not exactly our best friends on the planet either.

Even among our oil-producing allies, relations seem to have grown less amiable in recent years. Britain, which produces a sig-nificant amount of oil from the North Sea, joined the United States in the Iraq war, but the British population, along with much of Europe, was largely opposed to the campaign. Canada has always been a staunch ally, but recent trade disputes over soft-wood lumber have created noticeable resentment there.

Returning to Saudi Arabia, Doran concludes, "The United States has no choice but to press hard for democratic reforms. But the very attempt to create a more liberal political order will set off new disputes, which will inevitably generate anti-American feel-ings. Saudi Arabia is in turmoil, and—like it or not—the United States is deeply involved. As Washington struggles to rebuild Iraq it will thus find, once again, that its closest Arab ally is also one of its most bitter enemies." To this, we can add that one of our "most bitter enemies" is critical to our economic lifeblood. The bottom line is that the U.S. supply of energy, the most vital resource in our economy, is no longer as secure as it once was.

This sparks an obvious question: should we not be trying to develop alternative sources of energy?

Imagine, for instance, that your family's main source of food is a granary owned by your neighbors, but that there are two problems with the granary:

1. Some of the granary's owners hate your family.
2. The grain in the granary is not being replenished, so it will one day run out.

In that scenario, would it not be logical for you to start looking for other food sources, even if only as a backup? Would you not make it your top priority?

The failure of our society to put serious effort into developing alternative energy suggests that our leaders have made two errors of judgment. The first of these is to assume that since oil has always been plentiful, it will always be plentiful. As we will see in the next chapter, numerous civilizations throughout history have collapsed because they reached a limit on production of a crucial resource. Oil production is no different; it too has its ceiling. There is considerable risk involved in relying on the kindness of enemies, and ignoring the eventual peak and decline of oil.

The second error says there is no alternative to oil worth pursuing. This idea too, as we will show in later chapters, is false.

Unfortunately, the majority of society seems to have fallen into line and accepted these errors of judgment as fact. Unwilling to face reality, they cling to the faith that energy and oil are synonymous, and that the gas stations will always remain open, 24/7, pumping from a miraculously safe and inexhaustible supply.

3. Most serious, the world's demand for oil is growing faster than oil production can increase.

Some petroleum geologists, who subscribe to Hubbert's law, now believe that worldwide oil production may be close to its permanent long-term peak and will soon start to decline. Even if the peak is farther away than they think, demand for oil, especially from large developing nations such as India and China, is rising faster than production. If this trend continues—and we fully expect it will—the result will be an inevitable clash between supply and demand that will send oil prices soaring to unprecedented levels. On page 47 of *The Oil Factor*, I wrote, "Any way you slice it, oil seems headed for triple-digit levels by the end of the decade. Oil at $100 will be a minimum. Just to put this in perspective, this could mean gas prices at the pump approaching $10 a gallon."

Myopia on Wall Street

Curiously, my prediction of $100 oil attracted more attention than anything else I wrote in *The Oil Factor*. For a short while, I became "the $100 oil guy." Even though, by the time the book reached stores, oil had already risen to $50—a 250 percent increase from a few years before—most people seemed to find my prediction excessive, if not completely outrageous.

For my part, what I find most astonishing is how much in denial Wall Street remains regarding oil. Consider, for example, that the current bull market in oil has already resulted in price gains far greater than any we have seen in the recent history of financial markets. During the great bull market of the 1990s, it took the Dow Jones Industrial Average five years to double the first time, and another five years to double again. Oil, on the other hand, made its last major bottom in 1998 when it briefly touched $10 a barrel. Following that, it has moved steadily higher. By 2003, oil prices had reached $30 a barrel. As of this writing, oil fetches over $60 a barrel—more than double its price in 2003 and more than six times higher than its 1998 low. So oil has risen much farther, and much faster, than stocks did during the 1990s. Yet never during the 1998–2005 period did any major Wall Street firm project that oil prices would be higher one year forward. Wall Street is seemingly oblivious to the bull market in oil.

Of course, this bodes well for oil investors, since it implies that the prevailing bias toward oil is still negative. In other words, oil is a long way from becoming overbought, from reaching a peak. But it also shows us that Wall Street has become shortsighted in its understanding of oil. It has missed the start of a major trend in oil prices. What's more, Wall Street analysts are ignoring the realities of the oil industry.

Instead of recognizing the growing supply/demand squeeze, Wall Street has decided that commodities like oil have "normalized" prices. A normalized price is one that does not undergo long-term uptrends but rather fluctuates around the midpoint of a long-term, essentially flat trading range. This may have been true for oil in the 1990s, but not anymore. Nonetheless, normalized prices represent conventional wisdom. They are the authority of recent history.

Here is just one example from the A.G. Edwards brokerage, published in early March 2005, a time when oil was trading at well over $50 a barrel and oil futures contracts as far out as 2010 were trading in the mid-$40s. We pick Edwards because, during the early 2000s, they were much more bullish on oil stocks than most other firms.

"The market has quickly revalued the integrated oil group's normalized (mid-cycle) earnings, currently reflecting an oil price in the area of $35.00, on average, up from $24.00 last year, or a 46% increase (and from $30.00 just three weeks ago). And while we believe the group could now ultimately discount (or reflect) an oil price in the area of $38.00, it is our opinion, on average that the downside risk currently outweighs the upside potential. Based on a $28.00 mid-cycle oil price, downside is estimated at 23%, while the upside (based on $38.00) is only 6%."

It is difficult to explain the thinking behind this forecast. Here is a major, utterly credible brokerage firm defying all logic, defying the futures market, defying the facts expressed so clearly by all the major energy research organizations, and making pronouncements that have no basis in fact. In fact, as we shall see, the only way to explain such widespread denial of the facts is in the context of psychological phenomena that historically have led to major economic and political disasters.

In March of 2005, after the publication of *The Oil Factor*, Arjun Murti of Goldman Sachs caused some controversy by suggesting oil might exhibit a super-spike that would take it as high as $105. However, the nature of a spike is that it is brief. The price falls quickly back to where it started. Goldman Sachs still believes oil's long-term price will average between $30 and $40. A few other firms have grudgingly moved their long-term "normalized" price for oil as high as $50. Yet not one Wall Street analyst has dared to suggest that oil prices are in a long-term uptrend and that they will never be this low again. Pity any analyst who would challenge the consensus on this issue; he would quickly be looking for another job!

Myopia in Government

Unfortunately, refusal to look at the growing oil crisis extends beyond Wall Street. In chapter 3 of *The Oil Factor*, I referred to another article in the very reputable journal *Foreign Affairs*. Two passages in particular drew my attention because they dramatically illustrate the kind of doublethink that permeates authoritative opinion regarding energy today.

The article, written by Edward Morse and James Richard, appeared in the March–April 2002 issue. It concerns the impending battle for energy dominance between Russia and Saudi Arabia. These words appear on the third page: "Global demand for oil has been increasing by between 1.5 and 2 mbd [million barrels a day] each year, a rate of growth with alarming long-term consequences. The U.S. Department of Energy and the International Energy Agency both project that global oil demand could grow from the current 77 mbd to 120 mbd in 20 years, driven by the United States and emerging markets of South and East Asia. *The agencies assume that most of the supply required to meet this demand must come from OPEC*, whose production is expected to jump from 28 mbd in 1998 to 60 mbd in 2020. *Virtually all of this increase would come from the Middle East, especially Saudi Arabia*" (emphasis added).

Approximately twelve pages later, the article reads, "Riyadh, on the other hand, might have vast known reserves, but it also has a closed state monopoly. Most alarming, *Saudi Arabia has been unable for 20 years to increase its production capacity.* Nor is its position unique: *few OPEC countries in 2002 have more production capacity than they did in 1990 or 1980*" (emphasis added).

Juxtaposed, these two quotes are frightening. In order for the world to meet its future energy needs, the same countries that have been unable to raise their production capacity for more than twenty years must more than double their capacity over the next twenty years. Just how this amazing feat is to be accomplished, the article does not say. Even more frightening, however, is that the contradiction between the two passages went completely unnoticed by the authors. They, like Wall Street and oil company executives, appear to accept the authority of the world's two prominent energy research organizations, the U.S. Department of Energy (DOE) and the International Energy Agency (IEA), that if more oil is wanted, somehow it will be found and brought to market.

The conclusions reached in *The Oil Factor* are disturbing. A shortfall in energy supplies and an oil price of over $100 would have severe impact on our economy. However, since then we have come to believe that the most disturbing aspect of the situation is the failure of our leaders to recognize the problem and take responsibility for solving it. After all, why do the citizens of the world pay tax dollars to support the Department of Energy and the International Energy Agency? Surely it is so these agencies can give us an accurate picture of our energy supply, and help ensure that it can meet our needs over the long term. Surely it is the role of government to safeguard the long-term security and prosperity of the nation, not to give us patronizing reassurances or sweep genuine problems under the carpet.

If it is the case that these agencies, along with other authorities, have made serious misjudgments, it becomes vitally important for others to sound the alarm. So we will press on with our analysis, and see if the evidence for a growing oil squeeze has grown stronger or weaker since *The Oil Factor*.

Myopia in the Media

Having already quoted Wall Street analysts and government agencies, let us look at what the press has been saying about oil. Recently, our attention was drawn to the August 21, 2005, issue of the Sunday *New York Times Magazine*. The story was titled "The Breaking Point," and subtitled "Saudi Arabia, soaring demand and the theory of peak oil." As we mentioned above, Saudi Arabia is just about the only country anyone thinks can supply enough additional oil to meet the world's rising demand. Peter Maass, the author of the article, attempts to present a balanced view of the nation's oil reserves.

Maass begins with a clear statement that Saudi Arabian production will mean the difference between a world that can grow and one that could face horrible turbulence. "In the past several years," he writes, "the gap between demand and supply, once considerable, has steadily narrowed, and today is almost negligible.

The consequences of an actual shortfall of supply would be immense. . . . [It] could bring on a global recession. The impact on the American way of life would be profound. . . . The suburban and exurban lifestyles, hinged to two-car families . . . might become unaffordable."

Maass then asks, "But will such a situation really come to pass? To know the answer, you need to know whether the Saudis, who possess 22 percent of the world's oil reserves, can increase their country's output beyond its current limit. . . . Saudi Arabia is the sole oil superpower."

To answer his own question, Maass tries to evaluate the claims of energy banker Matt Simmons, author of *Twilight in the Desert*, who believes the Saudis are overproducing and may be on the cusp of a decline in oil output. Maass concludes that the evidence for or against Simmons's view is very murky. After all, no one other than the Saudis has enough information to make a reasoned assessment of their capabilities, and the Saudis have assured the world that Simmons is wrong.

In the interests of fairness, the article concludes by interviewing a retired chief geologist at Aramco, the Saudi Arabian company that controls the country's oil reserves. Sadad al-Husseini believes that the world is facing an oil shortage but is far less pessimistic than Simmons. The Saudis, he maintains, are not on the cusp of a catastrophic fall in oil production, but they will have a difficult time raising production enough to meet future demand. Maass implicitly accepts Husseini as a moderate and credible voice and warns that in the not too distant future we could be facing a shortfall of oil.

So the article is brave enough to say we must to do something about the oil situation, and that our politicians have been remiss in not dealing with the inevitable problem. But just when the crisis will arrive, Maass leaves up in the air. In other words, though the article is cautionary, it lacks a real sense of urgency.

And yet there is a contradiction at work here, because the data presented in the article, when juxtaposed, actually make a compelling case for an imminent crisis.

Here is what we mean. Maass notes, "Without the ability to flood the markets with oil, the Saudis are resorting to flooding the market with promises; it is a sort of petro-jawboning. That's why Ali al-Naimi, the oil minister, told his Washington audience that Saudi Arabia has embarked on a crash program to raise its capacity to 12.5 million barrels a day by 2009 and even higher in the years after that. Naimi is not unlike a factory manager who needs to promise the moon to his valuable clients, for fear of losing or alarming them. He has no choice."

So Maass is telling us that Naimi's promise of 12.5 million additional barrels per day of oil is certainly the upper limit of what the Saudis can do over the next four years and may in fact be an exaggeration. Now let us step back and examine this exaggerated promise of 12.5 million bpd. What does it imply for the world?

According to the article and other reputable sources, Saudi Arabia's current production capacity is approximately 10.5 million bpd. So the Saudis' crash program might add another 2 million bpd over the next four years.

Meanwhile, Maass cites well-known data that tells us worldwide oil consumption has grown from "79 million barrels a day in 2002 to 82.5 in 2003 to 84.5 in 2004." To this, we can add that the number for 2005 looks likely be close to 86 million bpd.

This means oil consumption has risen by 6 million bpd in the past three years—an average of 2 million bpd a year. If this trend continues, then the Saudis' crash program of 2 million bpd over four years—or half a million bpd per year—will hardly be adequate.

In other words, the article offers explicit evidence that we face a crisis, not in the indefinite future, but right now. The best-case scenario says the Saudis can supply less than 25 percent of the additional oil the world needs. Since Maass's whole premise is that the Saudis are the only hope the world has for satisfying its growing thirst for oil, we must infer that a serious energy crisis is at hand.

Why does Maass not point out this obvious conclusion himself? Why does he carefully place the crisis into an ambiguous, never-never land of a future? We suspect that, like most journalists, he feels an obligation not to cause panic. (Although if the media do not sound the alarm when a crisis is at hand, who will?) So he conforms to the misguided authoritative consensus that says oil is not an immediate problem.

We feel obliged to point out that the Department of Energy has recently revised its outlook for Saudi oil production. Instead of its former claim that the Saudis will raise their output to 14.7 million bpd, the DOE now thinks 14 million bpd is more likely. Yet even 14 million bpd is considerably more than the optimistic Saudi projection of 12.5 million bpd presented in the *New York Times Magazine* article. So if the Saudis are going to produce less than originally thought, how will global supplies be sufficient?

To answer that, the DOE has now decided that the former Soviet Union and the United States will both be able to produce more than originally thought. The agency assumes American production will rise by 7 percent over the next five years. That is a heroic assumption. U.S. oil production has been in decline for the past thirty-five years, just as Hubbert predicted. The United States has wanted to break that downtrend ever since it began. Yet, except for a small interruption when the Alaskan North Slope came online in the early 1980s—an interruption that lasted only a few years—Hubbert's law has so far stood firm.

We will have more to say regarding the former Soviet Union's chances of adding to worldwide oil supplies in a later chapter. For now, we will simply note that their recent burst of oil production, which started in the late 1990s, was nearly coincident with the advent of capitalism in the country. Indeed, there is a strong relationship between the former Soviet Union's oil production level and the stock chart of Yukos. Both have been disappointing lately.

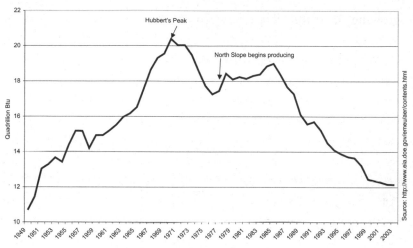

U.S. Oil Production, 1949–2003 (2002 and 2003 preliminary)

In addition, the DOE has a history of revising its projections of worldwide oil demand upward. Two years ago, it thought oil demand would reach 89.7 million barrels per day by 2010. The DOE's most recent prediction for 2010 is close to 95 million bpd.

In summary, all the evidence shows that the supply/demand squeeze I envisioned in *The Oil Factor* will actually be far more severe. An oil price of $100 per barrel by the end of the decade now seems a wildly optimistic prediction. Indeed, the only way oil will not top triple digits within the next few years will be if there is a huge worldwide depression. Moreover, even in the aftermath of such a depression, oil will very likely continue a dramatic uptrend that will result in prices well over $100—even if the "Hubbert's Peak" geologists are only half right.

We hope you understand the implications of what we have covered so far. The United States, and by extension the world, is facing the most serious energy crisis in history. It is a crisis for which we are completely unprepared, and that our leaders are not even willing to acknowledge. There is no plan in place to deal with a shortfall in oil production and very little chance of avoiding it, which means the economic consequences of this crisis will be dire.

If you find yourself disturbed by the idea that our society would ignore a problem of this magnitude, so are we. One has to remember, though, that it would not be the first time. Some would argue that recent disasters such as the technology crash, September 11, and Hurricane Katrina could have been foreseen to some extent, and that preventive steps could have been taken—if only our nation's leaders had been more open-minded and farsighted, if only they had paid more attention to the warning signs instead of basking in overconfidence.

We are not convinced that our society's leaders will respond to the threat of an energy shortfall in time to prevent widespread hardship. As we will demonstrate in the next chapter, civilizations throughout history have suffered catastrophic downfalls because of exactly the same type of situation we find ourselves in today—a shortage of a crucial resource, and a leadership unwilling to acknowledge or deal with the problem. Before it becomes too late, we must be willing to open our eyes.

CHAPTER 3

The Collapse of Civilization: Causes and Solutions

Before our society can put serious effort into preventing the approaching energy crisis, we must first understand just how high the stakes are. The technology bust dealt a serious blow to most investors. However, the results could have been far worse. Had we been a little less lucky, our nation might have suffered a major economic collapse—the kind that throughout history has caused not just widespread misery, but the end of entire civilizations. Unless we take preventive action, the approaching energy crisis could provoke just such a collapse within our lifetime.

That prediction may sound far-fetched. But actually, today's crisis is no different from those that have destroyed societies throughout history. One only has to compare maps of the world made in different eras to realize that nations come and go with astonishing frequency, and that civilization has always been a fragile enterprise. If we allow ourselves to become overconfident, we may be ill-prepared to deal with the next crisis to arise.

Of course, it is hard to accept the idea that our civilization could end. The United States has been in existence some 229 years. No one alive remembers a time before it. In addition, Western culture, along with the Judeo-Christian religions that have held sway for many centuries, has always encouraged us to believe our species has a special place in the universe. By extension, we tend to regard our civilization and our country as similarly special—and therefore less likely to collapse than cultures we think of as ancient, pagan, or otherwise inferior.

Science, on the other hand—an excellent tool for piercing our cherished illusions—reminds us we are not so special. Anthropology tells us that many of the fallen civilizations in history also thought they were superior to their neighbors and forebears. Few of their citizens could have imagined their society would suddenly collapse, just as few investors in 1999 believed technology stocks could collapse. Can we really assume that, after only 229 years, the United States is more secure than say, the Roman Empire, which lasted nearly a thousand years?

The Fragility of Civilization

Unfortunately, scientific estimates support the idea that our civilization is more fragile than we like to think. Michael Shermer, for instance, in a column for *Scientific American*, researched sixty civilizations, both ancient and modern.[2] His goal was to discover the life span of the average civilization. For each extinct culture, he calculated how long it remained in existence. For those still in existence, he used their current age.

Shermer concluded that the average life span of civilization is only 421 years. Even more jarring, modern civilizations do not last as long as ancient ones. Among the twenty-eight most recent civilizations—those that sprang into being after the fall of Rome—the average life span is only 305 years.

One reason may be that modern civilizations are more complex. By complex, we mean they have a well-developed division of labor, with most jobs requiring specialized skills and training, and

---

2. Michael Shermer, "Why ET Hasn't Called," *Scientific American*, August 2002.

that they have a hierarchical leadership structure, with various levels of government and other social institutions. Modern civilizations are also more likely to be in competition with other civilizations, so they demand more natural resources to sustain themselves and protect their territory. In other words, they are expensive to maintain.

Just because a civilization has been around for two or three hundred years, one cannot assume it will last forever. We have no special knowledge that tells us our civilization is more likely to endure than any other. The next crisis—which will likely be a shortfall in energy production—could be our doom.

The collapse of modern civilization would be a catastrophic event, far worse than the popping of the technology bubble. Never mind the financial hardship that would befall almost everyone—the end of our civilization, and its complex division of labor, would result in mass starvation and a level of violence and chaos not seen since the end of the Roman Empire.

If our civilization is to prevent such a future, we cannot allow the approaching energy crisis to catch us unprepared. We must discover the best strategy for preventing disaster, and implement it. We must learn the lessons of past civilizations—those that survived similar crises, and those that succumbed—and try to discover what actions will help us survive.

What We Know About the End of Civilizations

Fortunately for us, historians and archaeologists have spent a great deal of effort trying to figure out why civilizations collapse. Some general patterns have emerged.

The American historian Joseph Tainter in his 1988 book, *The Collapse of Complex Societies*, argues that the main reason complex societies collapse is that complexity—like other human endeavors—eventually suffers from diminishing returns.

Complex societies, according to Tainter, are problem-solving machines. They tackle one problem after another by marshaling a society's resources toward solutions. For example, the task of increasing the food supply may start with someone taking on a leadership role and winning the obedience of the population. Scientific study must be done to discover how to increase crop yields. An agricultural system must be developed. Farmworkers must be trained to follow it. Land use must be regulated. Production must be monitored, and the rules enforced. Food distribution systems must be created, so that some people can do the administrative work rather than farm labor. Administrators need special training and education. Effort must be made to maintain everyone's morale and faith in the leadership, through periodic celebrations or religious practices.

In the beginning, the problems a society tackles are those that are easiest to solve and bring the greatest rewards. So they are worth the effort and expense of maintaining a complex social structure. Over time, however, societies tend to move on to problems that are increasingly difficult and expensive to solve, so the rewards for solving them decline. Consequently, the cost of maintaining a huge bureaucracy, specialized professions, or upper classes grows increasingly burdensome.

According to Tainter, the essential currency with which a society finances its complexity is energy. Energy includes food supplies, human and animal labor, fuels (such as wood, fossil fuels, or uranium), and others. As long as energy is plentiful, a society can invest in more complexity. But once energy supplies reach their limit or start to decline, complexity becomes less and less affordable.

Eventually, a society may reach the point where trying to solve a new problem is not worth the cost. From then on, it becomes vulnerable. The next crisis or serious problem that comes along may be the straw that breaks the camel's back, and the civilization collapses.

For example, the Roman Empire began when Rome discovered it could increase its energy supply by conquering its neighbors and commandeering their grain production and labor (in the form of slaves) to sustain its own needs. At first, the system worked well. Rome became wealthy. However, with each new conquest came a greater need for complexity—a bigger civil service to run the empire, a bigger army to defend it, more education, public works, and social benefits for citizens. All of these required financing, either by taxes or by debasing the currency. Taxes eventually grew so high that many landowners abandoned their farms, causing food production to fall. In time, the costs of conquering new territories exceeded the rewards. Eventually, even defending the existing territory against barbarian invaders became too expensive. Rome, the predator, became the prey.

More than any other, Tainter's book inspired us to write this one. His emphasis on the importance of energy supplies seems eerily familiar when we look at today's world, where oil is becoming increasingly expensive and new reserves harder to find.

Yet we are not so fatalistic as Tainter. We believe civilizations can avoid collapse. The crucial element is the mind-set of the leaders, and how well they perceive and respond to problems.

The Failures of Leadership

Jared Diamond provides another way of looking at the downfall of civilizations in his book *Collapse*. Like Tainter, Diamond thinks most crises are caused by declining resources. However, for Diamond, whether or not a civilization survives such a crisis has more to do with whether its leaders make the correct decisions in time.

In his review of fallen civilizations, Diamond presents a picture of leaders who became so fixed in their traditional values that they were unwilling to alter them, even if it meant destruction. For example, one of the best-known examples of a collapsed society is Easter Island. Diamond describes in detail how, on Easter

Island, the ruling class developed a tradition of building enormous statues as a way of proving their legitimacy. The bigger the statue, the more status it gave the chief who had it erected.

Unfortunately, the process of erecting these statues required huge amounts of timber and rope (made from tree bark), not to mention human labor. As a result, over a period of three hundred years, the Easter Islanders cut down their forests until every last tree was gone. This drastically reduced their food supply. No more trees meant no more fruit, nuts, or other wild foods. It meant no more canoes with which to fish in deeper waters. And it caused soil erosion, which lowered crop yields.

Looking at the Easter Island collapse today, we cannot help feeling dismayed by the sheer stupidity of it. Did they not realize what they were doing? Could they not have abandoned their statue building in time to save their food supply? Diamond notes that even today's Easter Islanders have had a hard time admitting their ancestors were so shortsighted. Yet it seems the leaders of Easter were too entrenched in their ways to willingly change.

Diamond shows that similar attitudes explain the collapse of the Norse colony on Greenland. Like the Easter Islanders, the Greenland Norse unwittingly depleted their natural resources and degraded their environment. By cutting too many trees to create pasture for animals, they found themselves with a shortage of wood for heating their homes, for construction, and for smelting iron. By eroding their limited topsoil, they reduced the production of hay that fed their livestock, as well as their own food supply.

Yet apart from mismanaging their forests, the leaders failed in other ways to adapt to changing circumstances. Having come from Europe, the Norse maintained their tradition of raising dairy cattle, even though that contributed to the deforestation. (Dairy production requires large pastures and firewood for boiling water to sterilize milk containers.) The Norse believed in their own cultural superiority, so they failed to develop friendly relations with their neighbors, the Inuit, who could have taught them valuable new technologies to help them survive in Greenland's cold climate—technologies such as seal hunting, burning blubber rather than wood, making boats from sealskin, and more.

The Norse also clung to their religious practices. Traditionally, religion may have helped maintain social order. But unfortunately, as the colony's income from exporting walrus ivory declined (due to lower demand), the Norse continued to spend large sums on expensive church trappings, rather than on more useful imports such as iron that would have helped them survive.

From our perspective, it seems moronic that the Greenland Norse did not look at their growing problems and adapt a strategy that preserved their society. But like all ruling classes everywhere, these were people who likely had been trained from birth to maintain their social position. And that meant enforcing their society's traditional values. The Norse leaders would have felt as compelled to build cathedrals as the leaders on Easter Island were to build statues. They may have believed that to do otherwise would have opened the doors to short-term chaos and their own personal loss of rank.

We will have more to say in the next chapter about why focusing on short-term objectives is one of the worst mistakes a leader can make. For now, let us say that if leaders wait until a problem begins to seriously affect a society, it may be too late to solve it. Diamond suggests that by the time the last tree on Easter Island was cut down, saving it would have made no difference anyway. Trees had ceased to be a significant resource to the community.

Of course, had the Easter Island leaders been brave enough to consider the long-term health of their society, they might have risked introducing some reforms. Perhaps they could have tied a leader's status to the abundance of his forests, rather than the size of his statues. Similarly, if the Roman emperors had paid attention to the long-term health of the empire, they might have devised a nonmilitary solution to the food shortage. And the Norse leaders might have modified their religious beliefs to encourage more modest churches and cultural exchange with their neighbors.

Instead, lack of foresight and an almost childlike decision not to worry about the future seem to be human characteristics that are timeless. Ultimately, these psychological weaknesses may be more responsible for why civilizations have failed than resource shortages alone.

The Keys to Survival

We must point out that societies are not destined to collapse. Many have successfully coped with the problems of limited resources and remained intact. These survivors are beacons of hope that show us three reliable methods of survival.

First, faced with too high a price for increasing or maintaining complexity, a society can choose to become less complex. Of course, a decline in complexity is one definition of a collapse. However, there is a difference between a planned transformation to a simpler society and one that occurs against the leadership's will. The trick in either case is to make the transition without enormous loss of life.

In the early 1990s, the Soviet Union dissolved into a lower level of complexity. The reason is arguably that the Reagan buildup of military power in the West forced the Soviet Union to put its limited resources into either building an equally strong military or feeding its people. Keep in mind that as the need to finance burgeoning military budgets increased, so did the needs of maintaining an increasingly complex society and a government that spanned many republics. In the end, the Soviet Union chose a simpler form of government and granted autonomy to its formerly controlled states. This lowered the cost of government, while letting Russia keep enough military might to protect itself.

We cannot say the transition was without turmoil, but it could have been much worse had Gorbachev and other Soviet leaders been unwilling to take steps toward reform.

A second way of solving the problem of limited resources is for a society to adopt strict measures aimed at achieving a fixed but sustainable level of population, production, and consumption—a zero-growth society.

Diamond describes the success of the tiny South Pacific island of Tikopia. Living in near isolation for three thousand years, the Tikopians had to deal with the classic Malthusian problem of limited food production and the risk of overpopulation. And deal with it they did. They developed a complex agricultural system that maximized food production in a sustainable manner, and they created numerous population control methods that ensured their society never numbered more than around thirteen hundred people.

Another example of success is Japan, which in 1650 was on the verge of collapse due to deforestation, which (as is typical) was causing soil erosion and lowering crop yields. However, in less than a hundred years, Japan achieved a stable population and instituted a forestry management system that prevented disaster.

The third—and perhaps the most preferable—method of preventing a collapse is for a society to develop new energy supplies that allow it to maintain and even increase its complexity without becoming vulnerable to collapse.

For example, *The Doomsday Myth*, by Charles Maurice and Charles Smithson, describes how, in the sixteenth century, England warded off a potential disaster brought about by an energy crisis. At that time, the main energy sources for home heating and manufacturing were wood and its derivative, charcoal. Wood was also used extensively for home and ship construction. Unfortunately, Britain's forests were a limited resource that was being rapidly depleted. As a result, between 1500 and 1650, wood prices rose eightfold and England began importing wood at great cost.

What saved the day was that the British turned to a new energy source that (due to soaring wood prices) became economical—coal. Beginning in 1550, the British increasingly used coal in homes, workshops, and factories. This led to new methods of manufacturing, and the growth of various industries. As a result, by 1700 Britain had become the most productive economy in Europe. In fact, one could argue that the development of coal led to the Industrial Revolution and much of the prosperity the Western world has enjoyed since.

These examples show that reaching a production limit for a vital resource does not necessarily spell disaster. If a society can recognize the problem in time, develop a workable plan, and be willing to change its habits for the sake of survival, it can survive.

Yet we are still not completely satisfied with our understanding of why some civilizations fail to make the changes required to avoid collapse. After all, part of any leader's job description surely includes looking after the long-term survival of his or her people. Why do societies not replace shortsighted, closed-minded leaders with others who are willing to make tough decisions for the greater good? If the leadership chooses to ignore a growing problem, why do other members of society not sound the alarm and campaign for changes?

As it turns out, there are answers to these questions too. In fact, these answers not only explain the downfall of civilizations, but also the mistakes most individual investors made during the technology bubble. They also explain why today's growing energy crisis is being largely, perhaps fatally, ignored.

CHAPTER 4

Our Psychological Blind Spots: Conformity, Authority, and Groupthink

W e dislike the idea that our leaders may be too shortsighted to protect us from the approaching shortfall in energy production. Yet such a scenario has occurred too often in history for us to ignore the possibility. Similarly, the madness of the technology bubble disturbed us at the time, yet we know other speculative manias have occurred in the past, with similar tragic results.

It begs the question whether some flaw in human nature makes our leaders naturally prone to avoid tackling serious problems. Is civilization fated to experience periodic crises? Are investors genetically predisposed to be taken in by false promises? If so, will we be able to overcome our weaknesses in time to cope with the energy crisis?

Our Predictable Failings

Fortunately, we are not the first to question the human tendency to make serious errors of judgment. Following World War II, social psychologists attempted to understand how it was that German soldiers were induced to abandon morality and human empathy in order to commit the atrocities of the Holocaust. What they discovered, to everyone's surprise and dismay, was that the majority of people can be persuaded to do almost anything.

The first notable experiments were done by Swarthmore psychologist Solomon Asch. Asch wanted to discover whether people's tendency to agree with their peers was stronger than their tendency toward independent thought and rational judgment.

In one of his most famous experiments, Asch assembled a dozen or so Swarthmore students and announced that they were taking part in an experiment on visual perception. He showed them three line segments, and asked each one in turn which line was the longest. It was an easy task—the correct answer was obvious.

However, Asch had secretly instructed all but the last person, who was the real subject of the experiment, to say that the medium-length line was the longest. The aim was to see whether the subject would rely on his or her own judgment, or go along with the group. As it turned out, 70 percent of the subjects caved in to group pressure and said that the medium-length line was the longest. The conclusion was that most human beings, under conditions that are hardly severe, will follow the crowd, *even when the crowd is clearly wrong.*

Stanley Milgram, a former student of Asch, took this research a step further. Milgram wanted to see how much influence an authority figure could wield over the average person. In his most famous experiment, subjects were put in an artificial situation (although they believed it was real) in which an authority figure—a "scientist" in a white lab coat—instructed them to inflict pain on another person. In fact, those subjects who followed the instructions to the bitter end had reason to believe they were inflicting serious and even lethal pain on a fellow human being. Yet 65 percent of the subjects followed the instructions as given.

We must point out that Milgram selected subjects from all occupations and from various social backgrounds. They were not hardened criminals, soldiers, or mentally deranged. They were just average people. *Yet the Milgram experiments showed that most people's tendency to trust and obey authority is so strong that they will shed all personal responsibility, moral training, or creative volition for the sake of following orders.*

Taken together, the Milgram and Asch experiments explain much about how societies function. They tell us we have a natural tendency to let authorities think for us—to let them tell us what is true, moral, or the best course of action. Moreover, once a leader (or leaders) has convinced a sizable number of their followers to believe something, then our predisposition toward conformity tends to bring other group members on board.

When the Blind Lead the Blind

Of course, our tendencies to defer to authority and conform to our peers are not usually bad things. Most of what we do in life involves cooperating with other people. A group can work more effectively if its members "see" things the same way. Putting some people in charge because they have greater knowledge or skill, or because everyone trusts their judgment, can help a group achieve certain goals more efficiently.

Problems arise, however, when people's propensities to conform and to respect authority prevent a society from dealing effectively with a crisis. The most obvious example would be a society with a bad leader—one who refuses to acknowledge or deal with a growing problem.

Milton Rokeach, another notable psychologist who published extensively in the 1960s, believes that not everyone has a natural inclination to follow authority. In his book *The Open and Closed Mind*, Rokeach argues that there are two distinct personality types. Those who like hierarchies and are equally comfortable giving and taking orders are *authoritarian* personalities. Such people tend to be closed-minded in regard to new ideas and solutions. On the other hand, people with *open-minded* personalities are instinctively freethinkers who dislike authority, are interested in new ideas, and prefer to seek new, creative solutions.

Open-minded people have a broad perspective on time. They base their expectations for the future on a realistic appraisal of the past and the present. They develop theories from observing the world and look to see whether the future will confirm those theories.

Authoritarian people, on the other hand, have a narrow view of time. Their ideas about the past and future are highly idealized, and they have little sense of anything outside the present, or how the present might be changing. An authoritarian leader therefore tends to ignore growing problems until they make their effects seriously felt. Worse, the influence he wields as a leader can cause the majority of his followers to ignore the danger as well.

Of course, few leaders throughout history have been absolute autocrats. Most have been aided by groups of advisers whose purpose is to prevent the leader from making serious mistakes. However, evidence shows that such groups can themselves fall victim to psychological weaknesses that lead to serious misjudgments.

Social psychologist Irving L. Janis, building on the work of Asch and Milgram, shows why groups often make bad decisions in his 1972 book *Groupthink: Psychological Studies of Policy Decisions and Fiascoes*. Janis's main concern is the behavior within government policy groups, and how it can cause governments to choose a course of action that leads to disastrous results. At the time, he considered the Bay of Pigs fiasco of 1961 to be the perfect example of failed decision-making.

Janis recounts how the Kennedy administration's decision to train and equip a brigade of Cuban exiles, help them launch a military overthrow of the Cuban government, with American air support—all the while keeping American involvement a secret— was based on a number of incorrect assumptions. As a result, the plan failed miserably and wreaked major damage to American foreign relations for years afterward.

More significantly, Janis outlines how many of President Kennedy's advisers had had misgivings beforehand, had recognized that errors were likely being made. But the pressure to maintain group solidarity prevented those concerns from being properly raised and addressed. Some group members, Robert Kennedy for instance, actually tried to keep information from the president that might have alerted him to the danger.

Janis concludes that closed-mindedness, overconfidence, and pressure within the group to conform can lead to "a deterioration of mental efficiency, reality testing, and moral judgment," which he calls *groupthink*.

A recent parallel to the Bay of Pigs incident was the U.S. government's belief in the early 2000s that Iraq possessed weapons of mass destruction, a claim laid to rest by America's chief weapons inspector, David Kay, in 2004. The *Economist*, in a special report on the Senate Intelligence Committee investigation into the intelligence failure, notes, "It diagnosed a severe case of 'groupthink': that is, that the spies were failing to test the general assumption that Iraq had a growing WMD programme. To have done so would have been considered heresy; which may be why Hans Blix, the chief UN weapons inspector, accuses America of positing 'faith-based intelligence.'

"Thus programmed, America's spies tended to reject any intelligence that didn't support the thesis. Whatever did corroborate it, they embraced, with little regard to the credibility of the source. Accordingly, defectors who claimed that Iraq had abandoned its pursuit of nuclear weapons by the mid-1990s were dismissed as untrustworthy. Exiled opposition politicians and their relatives—including the dubious Ahmed Chalabi, who had not visited Iraq in decades—were considered more reliable."[3]

However, not all the blame can be laid at the feet of the CIA.

---

3. "Special Report: Intelligence Failures—The Weapons That Weren't," *Economist*, July 15, 2004.

In an article that strongly echoes Janis's description of the atmosphere within the Kennedy administration, former Clinton labor secretary Robert Reich describes the Bush administration as equally intolerant of dissent. He writes, "Operatives in the CIA suspected Hussein didn't have weapons of mass destruction, and personnel at the State Department knew the plan to invade Iraq was seriously flawed. But such judgments were suppressed by a White House that made perfectly clear what it wanted—and didn't want—to hear."[4]

We have no doubt the administrations of both Kennedy and Bush were staffed by people of fine intelligence and high ideals. Our point is that groupthink can affect any group trying to tackle an important job under stressful circumstances, and can lead to monumental errors of judgment.

Although groupthink primarily affects small groups, when a group or its members wield power and authority, their opinions can, through the phenomena we discussed earlier, infiltrate the entire society. And when the group members are the leaders of a society, such as a president and his cabinet, or any ruling caste throughout history, groupthink is even more dangerous. In such cases, a bad decision can have tragic results for the entire society.

We now have a much clearer picture of why civilizations collapse. Faced with a crisis, such as a limited supply of energy or resources, authoritarian leaders and groups afflicted by groupthink fail to make the right decisions for dealing with the problem in time. Most other members of society defer to these authorities, and the rest naturally feel the urge to conform. As a result, the entire civilization puts itself on course for disaster.

This is the situation we find ourselves in today. No authority—not Wall Street analysts, the media, government, or academia—believes that energy prices are in a long-term uptrend. Unless they soon realize that the mismatch between energy supply

---

4. Robert B. Reich, "The Paradox Explained," *American Prospect* 16, no. 10 (October 1, 2005).

and demand is a chronic and worsening problem, the resulting catastrophe will make the tech bubble look like a picnic.

Overcoming Our Psychological Barriers

We feel obliged at this point to let you know that we are not nearly as pessimistic as the above might suggest. We have painted a picture of our psychological weaknesses and how they contribute to the downfall of nations. But our purpose all along has been to help society, as well as individual investors, cope with the coming oil crisis. We think this purpose can be achieved.

Not all groups suffer from groupthink, just as not all civilizations succumb to collapse. Many individuals are open-minded enough to resist the pressure to conform, and are duly critical of authority. Forty-five percent of the subjects in the Milgram experiment stood up to authority and refused to follow instructions. Likewise, 30 percent of the subjects in Asch's experiment trusted their own judgment and correctly picked the longest line. For that matter, not everyone in the 1990s became caught up in the technology mania. And a few commentators today, us included, are attempting to sound the alarm about the oil crisis.

Moreover, we believe individuals can learn to become more open-minded. When we first wrote about Asch's experiments in a newsletter article, we received an e-mail from someone who had been a subject in one of them when he was a student. He was proud to say that he picked the longest line, despite what the rest of the group said. However, he noted that at the time he had not actually been a Swarthmore student. He attended Haverford.

In pointing this out, our reader was probably making a light-hearted jab at Swarthmore in the spirit of academic rivalry. Yet we could not help thinking he had a point. The fact that he attended a different school—that he identified himself as a member of a different group—may have meant he felt less pressure to go along with the Swarthmore crowd.

If, as individuals, we can learn to identify a little bit less with the herd, to question popular ideas and the pronouncements made by authority figures, and to develop our own conclusions, based on a broad range of evidence, then we may reach a level of emotional maturity that renders us less vulnerable to groupthink. We may become better equipped to think for ourselves, make good decisions, and take charge of our own destiny.

By way of analogy, when we are children, our parents may be the biggest authorities in our life. When we become teenagers, the opinion of our peers may become even more important. However, when we move into adulthood, we may learn to see things differently. We may recognize our parents' mistakes and their lack of wisdom in some areas. We may look at our peers with more objectivity. Then, if we are fortunate, we may start forming our own opinions, and making decisions that will better serve us in creating the life we desire.

As we will see in the next chapter, such emotional maturity also happens to be a requirement for becoming a successful investor—particularly in times of great change, such as today.

In addition, we believe it is important for society as a whole to develop emotional maturity and, along with it, the willingness to look at potential problems well in advance and to take steps to prevent the next crisis from becoming fatal to our civilization. We were lucky to survive the technology crash, but we cannot count on being lucky forever, especially since the coming energy crisis requires a very different solution than our leaders are used to applying.

If this book can, in a small way, either help inspire society to make the changes necessary to forestall the oil crisis or help individual investors prosper despite the crisis, we will be well rewarded.

CHAPTER 5

The Madness of Wall Street: How Investors Can Profit by Overcoming Groupthink

We now understand some of the psychological reasons why civilizations experience crisis and collapse. Human beings are instinctively inclined to let authorities think for them, and to conform to the opinions of the group. These instincts can lead people astray when the leaders of their society suffer from groupthink or authoritarian attitudes that cause them to be short-sighted and closed-minded concerning growing problems.

Coincidentally, this model also helps us answer the questions we raised in response to the technology crash. Earlier, we wondered how so many investors, both individual and professional, could have abandoned rational thought and analysis and let emotion stampede them toward financial disaster. We now surmise that too many "experts" and business leaders fell victim to groupthink. Hence, they based their projections of future profits from technology shares on the recent past, which was rosy, rather than on a more realistic, long-term understanding of how industries tend to mature. They brushed off any information that contradicted their projections, saying, "This time it's different." Individual investors then instinctively followed their leaders.

However, as tempting as it may be to blame the authority figures alone, we cannot absolve average investors of all responsibility. Nor would we want to, for if we believed people were inescapably ruled by their instincts, then we would all be forever doomed to repeat the same errors. We would be unable to protect ourselves from any future misguided path our leaders might set us on.

Fortunately, we believe that the ability to overcome our instincts and change our behavior is one our greatest gifts. While the technology crash had many victims, there were those who declined to follow the crowd, and emerged less scathed financially. We know too that many people can override their instincts toward conformity and deference to authority, that not all people are shortsighted and closed-minded.

The challenge for us, as investors, is to contemplate what other delusions may be widely held today as a result of groupthink. Then, in the process of dispelling these delusions, we can become better able to position ourselves on the right side of investment trends and developments. The history of the financial markets shows that those who follow the crowd often miss the most profitable opportunities, while the biggest gains go to those who think for themselves, distance themselves from the crowd, master their emotions, and are open-minded enough to see the big picture. In short, freeing yourself from groupthink can make you wealthy.

Conventional Mediocrity

Let us consider for a moment what advice investors typically receive. Most people, when they begin investing, turn to books or possibly investment advisers. Much of the advice given in books consists of rules or principles, and the rules most widely respected are those of Modern Portfolio Theory (MPT). Investment advisers are schooled in MPT as well, so most investors will be advised to follow it, one way or another.

A lot of academic research has gone into the development of

Modern Portfolio Theory, and much data assembled to support it. It is generally packaged as the most sensible, sober, and sound approach to investing. Some of the basic elements of MPT are:

1. *The Efficient Market Theory.* MPT assumes that the price of any stock, at any moment, reflects all information known about the company, and therefore is the best approximation of its true value. There are variations on this idea. The weak version is known as the Random Walk Theory, which states that since information about companies is released randomly, price changes are also random and unrelated to past prices. The strong version states that a stock's price reflects all private, insider information as well as public information.

The Efficient Market Theory also assumes all investors are rational, and so the market would never allow a stock's price to move out of line with its value. This implies that there is no such thing as an undervalued or overvalued stock, and no way to get superior returns by screening for value.

2. *Diversification.* Another key component of MPT was introduced by Henry Markowitz in his book *Portfolio Selection*. Markowitz argues that by diversifying an investment portfolio among several asset classes with different risk and return levels, it is possible to get the maximum return for a given level of risk. Today, investment advisers usually recommend that investors diversify their stock holdings into many different companies, industries, and other categories as well.

An important tool in designing a diversified portfolio is the Capital Asset Pricing Model devised by William Sharpe. This formula supposedly allows one to create a portfolio that will reliably outperform the broad market index during a bull market (and equally underperform in a bear market) by a predetermined degree. Of course, it assumes that the market performance and the volatility of individual stocks will resemble that of the recent past (more on this idea later).

If you are an institutional money manager, the great thing about MPT is that it makes your job easier. There is no need to look for undervalued shares, or worry about when to buy. The theory recommends buying and holding for the long term, so there is also no need to fret over market timing strategies. If your portfolio is well diversified, you should produce returns fairly close to those of the market—so no one can accuse you of doing a bad job, even in a bear market when share prices are plunging. And if you buy the same stocks every other manager buys, no one will criticize you for poor selection, no matter what your actual returns.

Modern Portfolio Theory is widely practiced by professional managers of pension and mutual fund portfolios. So you would think that if the theory was as sound as its reputation, portfolio managers on average ought to create returns higher than the broad index, which means higher than most other investors.

As it turns out, 75 percent of managers underperform the market, which means most investors would do better buying an index fund than buying a mutual fund. (An index fund, while never beating the market return, generally comes close to equaling it.) In fact, so many funds, as well as individual investors, experience poor returns that common wisdom (or folly) now says beating the market is impossible, except perhaps for short periods.

Yet we must keep in mind that market indices do not represent an impenetrable ceiling. Most indices are weighted averages—they represent the middle of the range of returns, not the top. To balance the stocks that underperform the index, there are other stocks that outperform. Similarly, there are investors whose portfolio returns are above average as well. Let us look at some of these investors, and see what kind of strategies they follow.

Extraordinary Individuality

The most successful living investor is arguably Warren Buffett. For the past thirty-seven years, the book value per share of his company, Berkshire Hathaway, has grown at a compound annual rate of 22.2 percent—well in excess of the market average. He has built a personal fortune of $44 billion, making him one of the two richest men in the world. Yet he has done it by following an investment strategy that is in some ways the very opposite of Modern Portfolio Theory.

Warren Buffett is above all a value investor. He carefully analyzes each company's financial situation and buys only stocks that are selling at prices below what he estimates they are worth. For his style of value investing to work (and clearly it does) the Efficient Market Theory must be invalid. Consequently, Buffett has said, "The disservice done students and gullible investment professionals who have swallowed EMT has been an extraordinary service to us."[5]

What is also remarkable about Buffett is that he does not diversify. Berkshire Hathaway's investment portfolio, which Buffett manages, is generally concentrated in no more than ten stocks at a time. In addition, Buffett does not diversify among industries or countries. For most of his career, he has stuck with American companies in the two industries he knows thoroughly—consumer franchises (such as Coca-Cola and Gillette) and corporate franchises (such as American Express). Buffett believes that the best way to reduce risk is not diversification, but careful stock selection, buying value, knowing everything about the companies you own, and holding for the long term.

As for Buffett's opinion of Modern Portfolio Theory, he once said, "Modern Portfolio Theory tells you how to be average. But I think almost anybody can figure out how to do average in fifth grade."

Another highly successful investor, whom *Money* magazine once noted was "arguably the greatest global stock picker of the

---

5. All quotations from Warren Buffett are taken from *The Warren Buffet Way*, by Robert G. Hagstrom, 2nd ed. (Hoboken, NJ: John Wiley & Sons, 2005).

[twentieth] century," is Sir John Templeton, founder of Templeton Funds. Before Templeton sold his stake (for $900 million) in the early 1990s, his company managed $23 billion in assets. Like Buffett, Templeton is a value investor. But unlike Buffett, Templeton is a global investor who will take advantage of a short-term economic trend and then move on.

For instance, Templeton began his career in investing while the United States was undergoing the Great Depression. In 1939, he borrowed $10,000 and bought $100 worth of every stock that was selling for $1 or less on the two biggest American exchanges. Out of the 104 stocks he bought, 34 were already in bankruptcy. Four years later, his initial investment had quadrupled.

When World War II ended, and most people were concentrating their portfolios on American stocks, Templeton saw an opportunity to profit in Europe. Convinced that the United States would help Western Europe get back on its feet, in order to prevent the spread of communism, he bought large European companies that had fallen in price because of the war. When the United States introduced the Marshall Plan to rebuild Europe, Templeton reaped big profits.

In the 1960s, when Japanese industry had a poor reputation in America, Templeton bought heavily into Japanese companies. However, by 1986, once Japanese companies had become household names, he sold most of his Japanese holdings and switched to resource-rich countries such as Canada and Australia. More recently, at the height of the 1990s technology bubble, Templeton sold short many of the leading dot-com and technology stocks, reaping another small fortune when the crash occurred.

In each of these examples, Templeton made money buying stocks that were unpopular and undervalued and selling them after they become popular and expensive. Clearly, his investment strategy was contrary to Wall Street groupthink and the opinions of most experts at the time—but that is why it worked. Let us share with you some comments Templeton made on his investing approach, which appear in *Global Investing the Templeton Way*, by Norman Berryessa and Eric Kirzner:

> We try to be apart from the crowd. You know you will never attain a superior record by buying the same stocks that the crowd is buying. You have to do something different.
>
> Let's assume that every securities analyst you see says, "That's the stock to buy!" You might think that if all the experts are saying "buy," you should. But you couldn't be more wrong. To begin with, if they all want it, they'll all buy it and the price will build up enormously, probably to unrealistic levels. By the same token, if all the experts say, "It's not the stock to buy," they won't buy it and the price will go down. It's then, if your research and common sense tell you the stock does have potential, that you might pick up a bargain. That's the very nature of the operation. It's quite simple; if everybody else is buying, you ought to be thinking of selling. But that type of thinking is so peculiar to this field that hardly anybody realizes how valid it is. They say: "I know you're supposed to look where other people aren't looking," but very few actually understand what that means . . .
>
> When greedy investors jump in to buy at the top of a bull market, I accommodate them by selling them my shares. When nervous investors are selling at the bottom, I accommodate them by buying.

Clearly, Templeton's advice would have been extremely valuable to investors near the height of the technology bubble, if they had been willing to listen to it.

Coincidentally, Warren Buffett has also stressed the importance of buying unpopular stocks: "We simply attempt to be fearful when others are greedy and to be greedy only when others are fearful."

Another great investor with a unique style is George Soros, co-founder of the Quantum Fund. Between 1970 and 1980, the Quantum Fund produced a return of 4,000 percent, and helped Soros's net worth reach a level of $11 billion.

Soros is particularly dismissive of the Random Walk Theory. He writes, "I have disproved it by consistently outperforming the averages over a period of twelve years. Institutions may be well advised to invest in index funds rather than making specific investment decisions, but the reason is to be found in their substandard performance, not in the impossibility of outperforming the averages."[6]

Soros developed a theory of market behavior that he calls *reflexivity*. Presented in his book *The Alchemy of Finance*, reflexivity proposes that business fundamentals and investors' expectations influence one another. On one level, trends in fundamentals cause investors' expectations to change over time. Traditionally it has been believed that if expectations (or stock prices) get too out of line with fundamentals, the fundamentals will force a correction in expectations (and prices).

Soros argues that, in addition, changes in investors' expectations can affect business fundamentals. For example, a high stock price can make it easier for a company to grow its earnings. Stock prices reflect both an underlying fundamental trend and the attitude or bias of investors. Conversely, as stock prices change, they can affect both the underlying trend and investors' expectations. Here is how Soros describes the boom/bust cycle:

> We start with an underlying trend that is not yet recognized—although a prevailing bias that is not yet reflected in stock prices is also conceivable. Thus, the prevailing bias is negative to start with. When the market participants rec-

6. All Soros quotes are from George Soros, *The Alchemy of Finance: Reading the Mind of the Market* (New York: John Wiley & Sons, 1987).

ognize the trend, this change in perceptions will affect stock prices. The change in stock prices may or may not affect the underlying trend. . . . In the former case we have the beginning of a self-reinforcing process.

The enhanced trend will affect the prevailing bias in one of two ways: it will lead to the expectation of further acceleration or to the expectation of a correction. In the latter case, the underlying trend may or may not survive the correction in stock prices. In the former case, a positive bias develops, causing a further rise in stock prices and a further acceleration in the underlying trend. As long as the bias is self-reinforcing, expectations rise even faster than stock prices. The underlying trend becomes increasingly influenced by stock prices and the rise in stock prices becomes increasingly dependent on the prevailing bias, so that both the underlying trend and the prevailing bias become increasingly vulnerable. Eventually, the trend in prices cannot sustain prevailing expectations and a correction sets in. Disappointed expectations have a negative effect on stock prices, and faltering stock prices weaken the underlying trend. If the underlying trend has become overly dependent on stock prices, the correction may turn into a total reversal. In that case, stock prices fall, the underlying trend is reversed, and expectations fall even further. In this way, a self-reinforcing process gets started in the opposite direction. Eventually, the downturn also reaches a climax and reverses itself.

The key point is that this entire boom/bust cycle results from investors having a flawed perception of the fundamentals. That flaw, we can theorize, is the result of the faulty thinking that emerges from groupthink and shortsightedness.

Soros used his theories to make money from the rise and fall of the conglomerate boom in the 1960s. The "flaw" at that time was that companies were growing their earnings through acquisitions rather than genuine business expansion, yet investors mistook it for actual profit growth.

Soros followed this success by investing in the rise and fall of real estate investment trusts in the early 1970s—buying at the beginning, when it was easy for REITs to generate both high income and capital gains. He sold his initial holdings for a good profit, and later made additional profits by selling REITs short as the end of the housing boom caused their share prices to plunge.

Two decades later, Soros became famous for "breaking the Bank of England," when he shorted the British pound. This action forced England to withdraw from the European Exchange Rate Mechanism, and earned Soros $1.1 billion in the process.

It would be tempting to call Buffett, Templeton, and Soros *contrarians*. Contrarian investing involves deliberately buying unpopular securities or selling popular ones. Yet that is too simplistic a term. None of these great investors engages in knee-jerk contrarianism. What they really are are independent thinkers. They carefully look for the most rewarding opportunities. It just happens that the best opportunities often involve taking advantage of the errors of groupthink.

Resisting Groupthink

Investing against the crowd requires more than just thinking for yourself. You may, through objective analysis, come to correct conclusions about an investment opportunity. But the tendency to conform is not strictly an intellectual process. It is largely emotional.

For example, suppose the investment crowd is moving in one direction, say by buying technology stocks. You may know rationally that they are making a mistake, and that you should either avoid that sector or sell it short. You may hear your friends or media experts give rational-sounding reasons why you should buy tech stocks, but if your knowledge and analysis are sound, you can easily counter their arguments with your own.

However, your instinct to conform to the group, to follow the word of authorities, is not rational; it is emotional. When you are betting against the crowd—especially when the crowd for a short time seems to be right—you may find that your confidence erodes. You may start to doubt yourself and your investment decisions. You worry that you are actually missing an opportunity and will end up poorer as a result. You want your share of the profits that everyone else seems to be making. It may be very difficult to resist abandoning what you rationally know is the correct plan and jumping on the bandwagon.

In short, sticking with your independent analysis means having to distance yourself not only from group opinion and group emotions, but also from your own emotions. It means developing awareness and mastery of your emotions—what is nowadays termed emotional intelligence.

We don't have time in this book to cover all the techniques by which investors can improve their emotional intelligence, but the essential key is to develop the habit of stepping back and observing the situation and your feelings objectively. We want to impress upon you the importance of developing this skill because it is essential for investment success. Almost all highly successful investors throughout history acknowledged that making money in stocks requires conquering one's instinctive emotional responses. So please consider the following comments from just a few of them:

From Warren Buffett: "Success in investing doesn't correlate with IQ once you're above the level of 125. Once you have ordinary intelligence, what you need is the temperament to control the urges that get other people into trouble in investing."

From Benjamin Graham (one of Warren Buffett's mentors): "The investor cannot enter the arena of the stock market with any real hope of success unless he is armed with mental weapons that distinguish him in kind—not in a fancied superior degree—from the trading public. . . . He must be relatively immune to optimism or pessimism and impervious to stock market forecasts."[7]

From Jesse Livermore: "It is inseparable from human nature to hope and fear. In speculation when the market goes against you, you hope that every day will be the last day—and you lose more than you should had you not listened to hope—to the same ally that is so potent a success-bringer to empire builders and pioneers, big and little. And when the market goes your way you become fearful that the next day will take away your profit, and you get out—too soon. Fear keeps you from making as much money as you ought to. The successful trader has to fight these two deepseated instincts."[8]

From Sir John Templeton: "It takes patience, discipline, and courage to follow the 'contrarian' route to investment success: to buy when others are despondently selling, to sell when others are avidly buying. However, based on a half century of experience, I can attest to the rewards at the end of the journey."

The Error of Shortsightedness

The other essential investment skill is to develop an open mind. You must accept that situations are always changing, and be willing to acknowledge that the recent past is not necessarily an accurate guide to the future. This alone will set you apart from the vast majority of investors. It can also bring you bigger than average rewards.

We noted above that professional money managers tend to use one of the components of Modern Portfolio Theory, the Capital Asset Pricing Model, to design portfolios that should produce the best possible returns for a given level of risk.

MPT and CAPM divide the potential risk/return of a stock

---

7. Benjamin Graham, *The Intelligent Investor* (1949).
8. According to Edwin Lefevre's book *Reminiscences of a Stock Operator* (1923).

into two categories. The first is called alpha, and refers to the risk/return of a stock that is independent of the market and general business conditions. The common practice of diversifying into twenty or more stocks of different industries tends to bring a portfolio's alpha to near zero. This helps create a portfolio that should, but does not necessarily, closely follow the index. Yet as the examples of many successful investors prove, the highest profits in any period may come from being concentrated in those stocks or industries that are experiencing the highest growth. Diversification is a risk-control tool for passive investors, but it does not improve returns for those who can spot the best opportunities.

The other category of risk/return is called beta. Beta refers to how much a stock tends to rise and fall with the market. A high-beta stock would tend to outperform in a bull market and underperform in a bear market. A low-beta stock is less affected by market trends. Betas are calculated based on a stock's recent history. In addition, when managers design portfolios they again base their assumptions about stock market returns on the recent past.

Yet betas change over time, as do market returns. As we have argued in previous chapters, to assume that the future will resemble the recent past is to have a narrow view of time. It is a shortsighted, closed-minded approach. In other words, it can be disastrous, because it will ignore the warning signs of major changes.

Of even more concern, according to research on behavioral finance, the tendency among investors toward shortsightedness is extremely common, and not just the result of using MPT. Richard H. Thaler, a leading researcher in this area, has found that, when making investment decisions, investors tend to weigh potential short-term losses more heavily than potential gains, even when they are expecting to stay invested for the long term. He calls this phenomenon "myopic loss aversion."[9]

---

9. Shlomo Benartzi and Richard H. Thaler, "Myopic Loss Aversion and the Equity Premium Puzzle," *Quarterly Journal of Economics* 110, no. 1 (February 1995): 73–92.

Other researchers have shown that myopia (or shortsighted-ness) can also make investors more likely to invest in certain securities, such as junk bonds,[10] and that investors who have made recent gains are more willing to buy riskier investments.[11] In other words, we have a natural tendency to expect the future to be like the recent past. Even more significant, professional traders appear to be more prone to making shortsighted investment decisions than are amateurs.[12]

One study, by Nicholas Barberis, looked at the market reaction when companies release positive news. The study found that the market tends to underreact to the first one to twelve months of good news from a company, and overreact to a consistent pattern of good news over a three- to five-year period. This of course defies the Efficient Market Theory, although it fits nicely with Soros's concept of reflexivity. Barberis concluded that a smart investor could make higher gains without higher risk by taking advantage of this pattern.[13]

These insights taken from behavioral finance support our premise that most investors enter the financial arena armed with the expectation that the future will resemble the recent past, that they make decisions based on that expectation, and that those expectations are not always rational. As Warren Buffett said in an interview in *Fortune* magazine (December 6, 2001), "Man's natural inclination is to cling to his beliefs, particularly if they are reinforced by recent experience—a flaw in our makeup that bears on

10. Thomas Langer and Martin Weber, "Myopic Prospect Theory vs. Myopic Loss Aversion: How General Is the Phenomenon?" *Journal of Economic Behavior and Organization* 56 (2005): 25–38.

11. Quoted in Richard H. Thaler, "The End of Behavioral Finance," *Financial Analysts Journal* 56, no. 6 (1999): 12–17.

12. Michael S. Haigh and John A. List, "Do Professional Traders Exhibit Myopic Loss Aversion? An Experimental Analysis," *Journal of Finance* 60, no. 1 (February 2005): 523–33.

13. Nicholas Barberis, Andrei Shleifer, and Robert Vishny, "A Model of Investor Sentiment," *Journal of Financial Economics* 49 (1998): 307–43.

what happens during secular bull markets and extended periods of stagnation."

Of course, there are times when the recent past can be a guide to future performance, such as in the middle of a trend. Trends can be very profitable to follow, particularly if you get in well before they end. However, most investors, being shortsighted, miss the start of trends and pile on near the peak. Similarly, most investors fail to recognize the start of a bear market. They hold their stocks, expecting that the previous bull will shortly resume, and end up taking big losses. In brief, shortsightedness causes investors to miss the key turning points, and suffer lower returns as a result.

On the other hand, investors who are open-minded enough to spot the turning points can enjoy vastly superior returns. Historically, the biggest fortunes are always made by those who bet on the right side during a period of change. Change is what creates the volatility and sharp moves that can alter a person's fortune overnight. Spot the next change right away, and you can become rich. But the longer it takes you to see it, the longer you stay on the wrong side, and the poorer you get.

That is of course what happened in the technology bubble. Many investors could not believe the market had reached a peak in the spring of 2000. It contradicted their expectations, so they held their stocks for many months as they steadily lost value. Meanwhile, those, such as Templeton, who sold tech stocks short made a fortune. Similarly, with Enron, Wall Street could not let go of its positive expectations for the company, even when it was obviously in trouble. Analysts continued recommending Enron shares right up until the day the company went into bankruptcy.

The Open-Minded Investor

To reap above-average investment gains, we believe you must shun groupthink and shortsightedness. You must learn to think for yourself, and be unswayed by emotion. Rather than enter the market with a set of expectations based on what worked or did not work in the recent past, you must remember that the situation is always changing—conditions were different before the current trends began, and they will be different in the future. Your task is then to have a long view of history, to look at the present and try to discern where things are likely to head next. You must also be willing to revise your opinion as things change.

It is worth noting that George Soros conceives of the market itself as very like an open mind—a testing ground for ideas: "The markets themselves can be viewed as formulating hypotheses about the future and then submitting them to the test of the actual course of events. The hypotheses that survive the test are reinforced; those that fail are discarded. The main difference between me and the markets is that markets seem to engage in a process of trial and error without the participants fully understanding what is going on, while I do it consciously. Presumably, that is why I can do better than the market."

As you will see in later chapters, the market at the moment is testing the hypothesis that oil prices will remain stable over the long term. That is the premise being preached by authorities and those affected by groupthink. Consequently, stocks are priced and funds are allocated based on this assumption. We believe enough evidence exists to prove this premise is false. In addition, we believe the coming oil crisis will be the biggest test our civilization has ever faced, thanks to a shortsighted leadership that has taken few steps to prevent it.

However, we will conclude this chapter with two rays of hope. One is that we believe investors can profit immensely from the changes that are taking shape in the world, even if the oil crisis turns out as severe as we expect. In later chapters, we will tell you exactly how to make money from the situation.

The other source of hope is an observation by George Soros that a prevailing bias in the market—groupthink, in other words—often prevents its own prophecies from becoming true. In other words, when everyone believes a disaster is looming, they tend to take actions that prevent it.

Soros writes, "Perhaps some of the developments I predicted were preempted by the very fact that they were anticipated by the market and the market provoked a reaction that prevented them from happening. . . . When I finally recognized that markets can preempt the catastrophes they predict, I concluded that we live in an age of self-defeating prophecies. . . . It is an old joke that the stock market has predicted seven of the last two recessions. . . . By the same token financial crashes tend to occur only when they are unexpected."

If everyone in the world believed the price of oil would soon reach $200 a barrel, precipitating a serious crisis, it would probably never happen. That belief alone would cause the world to take massive steps toward energy conservation and developing alternative energy sources. As a result, the supply/demand squeeze that threatens to bring about $200 oil would be eliminated. In our opinion, that would be the best-case scenario.

We confess that part of our aim in writing this book is to help create the widespread belief that an oil crisis is imminent, so that society will take steps to prevent it from happening. Our greatest hope, therefore, is that the predictions made in this book will turn out to be wrong, because that will mean society became clear-sighted in time.

At the same time, we know it is unlikely that this book alone will change society. So while we hope it will make an impact, we're not counting on it. Meanwhile, however, we are confident that at least we can help individual investors grow wealthy from the events we predict.

CHAPTER 6

The Most Dangerous Crisis of All

We hope our previous chapter has convinced you of the benefits of becoming a more open-minded and emotionally intelligent person, at least in your investment career. We hope so, because that trait may be an absolute prerequisite for financial success in the developing oil crisis.

Like most great civilizations, ours has a strong belief in its own permanence. It is confident in its ability to survive any challenge, and it believes its values and ideals are superior. Naturally, we want our civilization to continue well into the future. We have a vested interest in it.

Yet an objective view of history tells us that there really are no guarantees. We know that civilizations collapse regularly. And with only 229 years under its belt, we also know our American civilization is too young to have demonstrated any special advantage that will guarantee its long-term survival. It may last another nine thousand years, or perhaps only another six.

The coming oil crisis could well be the biggest challenge our nation has ever faced. The question we must ask, therefore, is whether our civilization has developed the wisdom and skills needed to overcome it. What have we learned from our most recent brushes with disaster? And are these lessons adequate to the task of helping us survive the approaching crisis, especially since this crisis will be very different from those that have come before?

What Our Civilization Has Learned from Recent Crises

Over the past hundred years, the United States has successfully pulled through a number of close brushes with disaster. Because of these experiences, our leaders have acquired the habit of responding to each crisis with a large, fast infusion of financial liquidity.

The first big lesson came from our government's mishandling of the Great Depression, one of the most dangerous crises we have ever faced. Most people view the stock market crash of 1929 as the beginning of the Depression. Yet the crash alone was really not a big deal. Other market crashes in recent times have been far more severe. In October 1987, for example, the averages plunged farther and in less time than in 1929. Moreover, the '29 crash was followed by a stunning market rally in 1930. From its 1929 low to its high in the first quarter of 1930, the S&P 500 climbed about 50 percent. That ranks among the greatest rallies in market history.

In other words, the market crash of 1929 was more a warning than a cause of the Depression. As in 1987, it drew attention to the vulnerability of the economy and the need for drastic action to save the day. But what caused the Depression was our inability to find the right medicine for curing the economy.

At the time, experts generally believed that capitalistic economies gravitate to a natural equilibrium of full employment. Therefore, the government's role in the economy is to do as little as possible. So President Hoover tried to restore business confidence by balancing the government budget, hoping the economy would then recover on its own. Unfortunately, this policy only reduced demand for goods, and contributed to the economy's collapse.

The government also imposed trade restrictions in order to boost demand for domestically produced goods and help American companies compete with imports. Unfortunately, this too only made the economy weaker. Clearly, conventional wisdom was not working.

When Roosevelt won the presidency in 1932, he introduced government spending programs in the form of the New Deal, which are generally credited with curing the Depression. Nonetheless, the New Deal was likely motivated by compassion and political expediency rather than economic insight, and the liquidity it provided proved inadequate. By 1940, more than one in five non-farmworkers remained unemployed. Real wages (after adjusting for the decline in prices) were 10 percent less than a decade before. In other words, ten years after the Great Depression began, the United States was still reeling.

In 1936, John Maynard Keynes argued in his book *The General Theory of Employment, Interest, and Money* that in times of depression, government spending needs to compensate for insufficient business investment. His ideas attracted a few people, including Amadeo Giannini, the legendary builder of the Bank of America. Harold Evans, author of *They Made America*, notes, "He [Giannini] did not join the line of lemmings, marching over the cliffs as they intoned the slogans of the balanced national budget; Giannini, like John Maynard Keynes, saw that deficit spending to put money in people's pockets was imperative in a depression characterized by lack of demand." But Giannini was an exception.

Today we know that the right medicine in times of economic contraction is to spend like crazy and pump the economy full of money. But we did not do that in the 1930s. The spending programs that comprised the New Deal may have been a step in the right direction, but they created a budget deficit far smaller than what Keynes recommended. Because of that, they were unable to pull the economy out of depression.

Instead, what really ended the Depression and saved the United States from continued economic malaise was World War II. While America did not enter the war until 1941, Europe's entry in 1939 resulted in a flood of orders from abroad for armaments and other war necessities. It was these orders that started putting America back to work, not the New Deal or any other purely economic measures that had been enacted up to that time. With America's entry into the war, government spending finally reached the level Keynes had advised, and pulled the American economy out of the Depression.

Perhaps it was a mere lucky fluke that a war began at the right time to rescue the American economy. But there was nothing haphazard about America's handling of the Second World War, once we chose to enter it. We are not going to discuss the entire history of World War II, but it is clear that the United States created a plan for winning it—a plan that made sense. The nation executed that plan, if not perfectly, at least successfully. Perhaps

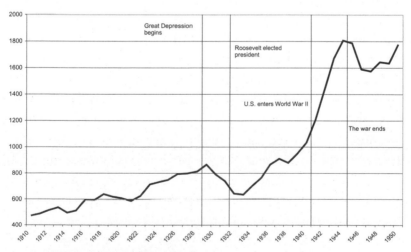

U.S. Real GDP, 1910–1950 (2000 US$)

the best example of planning and execution was the Manhattan Project, the four-year crash program that was set up to develop an atomic bomb. We managed to recruit the best and brightest minds to that project. And the results showed how successful focused and intelligent planning could be.

Winning the war was, of course, much more than the Manhattan Project—it was the successful mobilization of an entire country's resources. It is estimated that the war cost the country, in today's currency, more than $1 trillion. Coincidence or not, we will see in chapter 11 that $1 trillion is roughly the sum we will need to spend today to solve our growing energy crisis.

Regardless, the experience of the Great Depression and World War II taught America a clear lesson: spending and creating liquidity is the way to stave off a severe economic decline, not balancing the budget.

After the Japanese stock market crash in 1990, America had the opportunity to watch another society struggle with a major downturn in its economy. The Japanese had the advantage of being better schooled in Keynesian economics. So they tried stimulating their economy by lowering interest rates and eventually running huge government deficits.

Unfortunately, monetary stimulation brought a much smaller benefit to the Japanese economy, which has taken considerably longer to recover than did the United States. Some, such as former Federal Reserve chairman Alan Greenspan, have argued that the Japanese authorities took too long to respond to economic weakness. Perhaps that is true. Yet it is also true that the Japanese consumer saves a huge chunk of his income, whereas Americans have very low savings rates. Consequently, economic stimulation was less effective in Japan than in the United States, where monies gained through lower taxes and interest rates were quickly spent.

Whatever the case, by the time the technology crash occurred, our leaders had concluded that the secret to preventing an economic disaster is a fast increase in financial liquidity. That was the

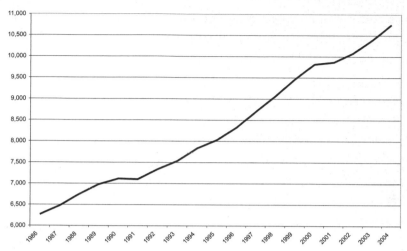

U.S. Real GDP, 1986–2004 (2000 US$)

plan they followed, and it worked. We were lucky to have learned this lesson, and perhaps lucky that our propensity to spend is high. Our dramatic response to the bursting of the tech bubble in 2000 and the terrorist attacks of September 11, 2001, turned what could have been a catastrophic depression into a relatively mild recession.

But we must not get too proud of ourselves, or too complacent. There is more to the story . . .

What We Have Not Learned

As we pointed out in previous chapters, one reason civilizations fall is that they do not take steps far enough in advance to prevent a crisis. That is one difference between medicine and economics. In medicine, we know we will eventually experience a life-threatening disease or a deteriorating body. We also know that many of the cures and treatments for serious diseases come with unpleasant side effects, and often do not restore us to full health. So we can see the value in taking steps today to delay illness, or prevent it from ever occurring.

Unfortunately, citizens of most complex societies typically feel too optimistic about their civilization's survival. They see no need for preventive medicine because they have no real sense that their economy could die. Consequently, they often pay little attention to problems until they become severe enough to threaten their present lifestyle. Of course, by then it might be too late.

Modern civilization has been lucky so far, in that the crises it has had to deal with have been the kind that we could solve with money. Both the American and the Japanese depressions were cured by higher government spending and liquidity. True, it took a while before the solutions arrived, and both depressions were painful. One can also argue that the depressions might have ended sooner if policymakers had used the right tools from the outset, or acted more quickly. However, in the end the Japanese and U.S. economies still survived. And perhaps it was lucky that the solutions took hold before the damage became too great and the entire civilization had begun to unravel.

It was also lucky that their examples prepared us well for dealing with the technology crash of 2000. Without that quick infusion of liquidity, the aftermath could have been far worse.

Imagine for a moment what might have happened after 2000 if the Federal Reserve Bank and federal government had not acted as quickly as they did. Suppose there were no tax cuts in 2002 and that the Federal Reserve had waited too long before lowering interest rates. Most likely, in the wake of 2001, consumers would have been unwilling to spend. Indeed, if the government had not dropped interest rates and cut taxes as quickly as it did, consumers would have had much less money to spend. The fall in consumer demand would have resulted in higher job losses and a recession far more severe than the one we had.

We were lucky things turned out so well in the early 2000s because, though we reacted very quickly and with the right strategy, we still did not react until the threat—the stock market crash and September 11—began to affect our present living conditions. But even if we had waited, we would arguably still have been in a crisis that we could have solved with money. Even if consumer confidence had been shattered, as in the case of the Great Depression, enough money might still have saved the day. (It would have just meant a longer and more painful haul.)

The problem is, unfortunately, that not every crisis can be solved with money—at least not quickly. Fast cash will not solve a shortfall in a vital resource such as energy. In such cases, it takes time to put a workable solution in place. When a society like Easter Island or Tikopia faces declining food production, waiting until everyone is starving is a fatal error. At that stage, desperate people will simply consume whatever resources are left until society collapses. It is far better to begin putting solutions in place—such as conservation or developing new supplies—before the problem becomes severe, and while enough resources remain to tide society over until supply can balance demand once more.

Today, the United States faces several growing problems. Some of these, such as the widely discussed Social Security crisis, are problems that might be solved with money. The U.S. government budget deficit and the trade deficit are massive problems that may result in a falling dollar and eventually a lot of inflation. However, inflation, while it may make us poorer, is unlikely to threaten our way of life significantly. In the end, we would argue that these too are crises that might be solved with money.

But the inevitable ceiling, followed by a decline, in energy production is a problem that cannot be solved with a quick infusion of cash. Solving it will take not only massive amounts of money but also many years of work developing alternatives. Failing to solve it could spell disaster for our civilization.

In later chapters, we will describe in more detail the seriousness of the developing oil crisis, and the steps our civilization must take if we are to survive it. But for now, let us just remind you that our society has had advance notice of this crisis for some time, yet has made little effort to prevent it.

Joseph Tainter wrote in 1988 that energy is a requirement of complex societies. The more complex the society, the more energy flow it needs. Our society is the most complex ever created, which makes large amounts of energy all the more essential to maintain it. Consequently, Tainter states, "Recent history seems to indicate that we have at least reached declining returns for our reliance on fossil fuels, and possibly for some raw materials. A new energy subsidy is necessary if a declining standard of living and a future global collapse are to be averted. A more abundant form of energy might not reverse the declining marginal return on investment in complexity, but it would make it more possible to finance that investment."

Going back even farther, to 1969, Buckminster Fuller issued a warning about the inevitable future shortage of oil and the need to develop renewable energy in his book *Utopia or Oblivion*: "There are gargantuan energy-income sources available which do not stay the processes of nature's own conservation of energy within the earth's crust 'against a rainy day.' These are in water, tidal, wind, and desert-impinging sun radiation power. The exploiters of fossil fuels, coal and oil, say it costs less to produce and burn the savings account. This is analogous to saying it takes less effort to rob a bank than to do the work which the money deposited in the bank represents. The question is cost to whom? To our great-great-grandchildren, who will have no fossil fuels to turn the machines? I find that the ignorant acceptance by world society's presently deputized leaders of the momentarily expedient and the lack of constructive, long-distance thinking—let alone comprehensive thinking— . . . render dubious the case for humanity's earthian future."

Of course, very little heed was paid to Fuller's warning. Since oil has always seemed plentiful and far less expensive, developing renewable energies was regarded as a very unrewarding enterprise, except to a few radical environmentalists who support the idea on moral grounds. That is, except for a brief period in the late 1970s when America received a taste of what the eventual oil shortage would be like.

In 1973, because of the Arab-Israeli war, OPEC imposed an embargo on oil exports. This caused energy prices to soar and produced long lines at gas pumps. Higher gas prices resulted in a worldwide economic slowdown and a lower demand for oil, which began to bring oil prices down. But then in 1978, the Iranian revolution provoked a second oil crisis and pushed oil prices to a level nineteen times higher than at the start of the decade.

The huge gains in oil prices made Americans realize what a world of declining oil supplies would look like. As a result, President Carter made a speech on July 15, 1979, in which he proposed a campaign to reduce America's dependency on foreign oil. In addition to promising that the United States would never increase its foreign oil imports from that time forward, he announced plans to develop alternative fuels and reduce energy consumption.

Yet the energy crisis of the 1970s was really just a political crisis, not a crisis of supply. The world still had plenty of ability to increase oil production. So when the political crisis ended and some new nuclear power plants came online, resulting in lower energy prices once more, everyone stopped worrying about energy. America quickly returned to its old spendthrift and gas-guzzling ways. Oil consumption in the United States bottomed in 1983, but between 1985 and 2000 it doubled. During that same period, use of renewable energy hardly increased at all. Automobiles, thanks to the growing popularity of SUVs, are less fuel-efficient today on average than they were in the 1980s. Since 1994, the United States has imported more oil than it produces.

Meanwhile, the world's oil reserves have not increased a great deal, most likely because there is little left to find. The bottom line is that we are more vulnerable to an energy shortfall today than we ever were.

Clearly, we have not paid attention to the early warnings about energy supplies. Our political leaders may have learned how to deal with an immediate crisis, at least one that can be solved with fast cash. But they have not learned to take preventive measures well in advance of a crisis. We have made little effort to free ourselves from our dependency on oil.

In the past five years, oil prices have more than tripled. Soon we may reach the point where rising energy costs begin to threaten our way of life. We need new energy sources if our civilization is to remain in its current form. Yet it may take decades to bring alternative sources online, and if we do not act soon, what will become of our way of life?

Unlike Tainter, we do not believe that a limit on oil production alone is enough to cause the downfall of our society or force us to downsize our complexity. Rather, we believe the biggest obstacle is groupthink. In particular, we believe our society's leaders, in government, Wall Street, academia, and elsewhere, are ignoring the hard data about the oil situation, and have adopted the false belief that enough oil will "magically" appear when we need it. A second delusion, equally dangerous and widely held, is that alternative energy sources are insufficient, uneconomical, or otherwise not worth the effort to develop.

Our society needs to become open-minded enough to acknowledge the growing energy problem before it is too late. It needs to change its attitude regarding alternative energy and take steps to bring new energy sources online before the crisis grows acute. It may be very difficult for our society to renounce its false beliefs, as they are grounded in groupthink and shortsighted, authoritarian attitudes. But, as you will see, not to do so would be to take us down the same misguided route to collapse that extinct civilizations have followed throughout history.

Those may seem like strong words, but after looking as objectively as we can at the data, this seems to us the most likely conclusion.

How Much Time Is Left?

In the next two chapters, we will show why energy prices will likely reach levels many times higher than most experts expect, and the difficulties this will create for both government policymakers and individuals. For now, let us conclude by pointing out that the crisis could arrive full-blown in a very short period of time.

The French mathematician René Thom developed a mathematical model known as Catastrophe Theory that explains why sharply discontinuous events often happen in the natural world. His work shows how stress can build up in a system to the point where it becomes unstable. From then on, the odds of a sudden, unexpected breakdown increase. Catastrophe Theory fell out of favor because it cannot predict exactly when a breakdown will occur. The only solution is to prevent stress from building to a dangerous level.

In the past few years, we have seen a number of unexpected events place greater stress on our economy—from the attack on the World Trade Center to Hurricane Katrina. The question is, will our society be astute enough to make the necessary decisions now to relieve the supply/demand pressures on our energy supplies, before the next big stress provokes a sudden breakdown of the entire system?

The energy crisis will be the biggest problem our civilization has ever faced. And it is vital that our leaders, and society as a whole, wake up to the situation and take preventive measures in time.

CHAPTER 7

Chindia and the Future of Oil

The biggest question most people ask us when we talk about oil is, "Just how high could oil prices go?" We have already hinted that *The Oil Factor*'s prediction of $100 a barrel now seems too conservative. So now let us try to extrapolate from what we know today and see where it takes us.

In late 1998, oil reached a low of about $10 a barrel. Six years later, the price had climbed to about $50, and in recent months it has gone as high as $65. There are several reasons for that huge gain, but the simplest explanation is that there is a mismatch between supply and demand. While OPEC and Russia have added to the world's supply of oil during recent years, demand has grown much faster. More significant, we see no signs that the factors that have been driving oil prices higher are lessening. On the contrary, if anything, they are growing more intense. Consequently, we expect the current uptrend in oil prices will accelerate.

Keep in mind that worldwide economic growth between 1999 and 2004 was not terribly high. In fact, the annual growth for the period was less than 3 percent. That is nearly one percentage point, or more than 30 percent, lower than the average annual growth throughout the post–World War II period. So we cannot explain the surge in oil prices as resulting from a sudden explosion in growth—far from it. But if raw growth cannot account for the oil price hike, what does?

Clearly, what drove the recent surge in oil was the inability of oil producers to keep up with unexpected gains in demand. This new demand, while not off the chart, was considerably greater than you would have expected if you had simply studied the raw growth numbers. Historically, growth in demand for oil has been roughly half that of economic growth. But in the 1999–2004 period, demand was more than 65 percent of growth. What changed the relationship? It was that world growth was not led by the developed countries, as has been the case for most of the post–World War II period. Instead, world growth is now being led by the developing countries—in particular by China and India, or what we term "Chindia."

In addition, this new relationship is not going to change for a long time to come. The per capita consumption of virtually everything in Chindia, from energy to computers, is a small fraction of what we find in the developed world. Yet with 35 percent of the world's population living in Chindia, even that small per capita consumption has a large impact, so much so that in the past decade Chindia's economy has grown to the point where it consumes nearly 90 percent as many goods and services as does the United States. That makes it a major player on the world stage. Moreover, with a growth rate that is two to three times higher than the United States, Chindia will likely surpass the United States in consumption before the end of this decade.

Let us explain how we arrive at these figures. When we say Chindia consumes 90 percent of what the United States does, we are talking in terms of purchasing power parity (PPP), as opposed to the dollar value of the goods and services consumed. PPP is a concept used by economists (and in this case our source is the World Bank) to compare economies without regard to the value of their currencies.

For example, if you were to compare two homes with the same

square footage and amenities in Iowa and Westchester, the West-chester home would probably be more expensive in terms of dollar value. Yet in terms of actual goods, the homes would be the same.

PPP is a better indicator of how important an economy is to the world because it objectively measures how much energy and other commodities that economy will need to sustain itself and to grow—just as the size and type of a house is a better indicator of how much furniture it needs than its price. The fact that Chindia, which is still a developing and in many ways an immature econ-omy, is nearly as large as the United States is a very big deal.

Let us explain. Suppose there are only two cities in the world. The first—which we will call Smallville—is one-tenth the size of its neighbor, Largeville. But Smallville is doubling in size every year, while Largeville is not growing at all. The size of the world (measured as the number of Largevilles) is 1 plus ⅒, or 1.1. After one year, Smallville has doubled, so the size of the world is 1.1 plus ⅒, or 1.2. In other words, the world has grown by about 9 percent (the difference between 1.1 and 1.2).

So far, Smallville's growth has not made much difference to the world economy. However, as time marches on, Smallville's impor-tance grows dramatically:

Year	Size of Largeville	Size of Smallville	Total world economy	Increase in world economy
0	1	0.1	1.1	0% (base case)
1	1	0.2	1.2	9%
2	1	0.4	1.4	17%
3	1	0.8	1.8	29%
4	1	1.6	2.6	44%
5	1	3.2	4.2	62%
6	1	6.4	7.4	76%
7	1	12.8	13.8	86%
8	1	25.6	26.6	93%
9	1	51.2	52.2	96%
10	1	102.4	103.4	98%

As you can see, after ten years, Smallville will have grown to 1,024 times its former size and the entire world will be 94 times larger than it started. Now we find that Largeville has become irrelevant. Moreover, the following year, when Smallville doubles again, the world economy will effectively double as well.

From our little example, we can derive a general principle. If you have two or more quantities, regardless of their starting size, the fastest-growing one will eventually dominate. In addition, the growth rate of the fastest-growing one will eventually approximate the growth rate of the whole.

This scenario is unfolding today between the Western world and Chindia. Chindia is the fastest-growing part of the world in terms of virtually any economic variable, from computers to copper to oil. Moreover, Chindia's low per capita consumption of all these products means this fast growth rate should be sustainable for perhaps a generation or more.

Take energy, for example. Chindia currently consumes, on a per capita basis, half as much energy as the entire world and one-seventh as much as high-income countries. If Chindia were to become a member of the high-income group within the next twenty years—even if we assume virtually no growth in energy demand in the rest of the world—then the worldwide growth in energy demand would rise to over 5 percent a year. That is far higher than any growth rate we have ever witnessed in modern times.

So let us return to our earlier question. What has changed since the end of 1998? The major change has been that Chindia has become a larger portion of the world. And as a larger portion of the world, Chindia is causing worldwide demand for all forms of energy, including oil, to accelerate. Thus, simple extrapolation tells us that oil prices will continue to accelerate because of greater growth in demand.

Today, developing countries—including Chindia, with its massive energy needs—make up a far more significant part of the world economy than they did in the 1970s. In this context, we must consider that the dramatic jump in oil and gasoline prices that occurred in 2005 is only the first sign of what will be a generation-long upward trend. Unless our society takes drastic action to alter this trend, oil and gasoline will simply not return to any kind of stable price range, or get any less expensive, ever again. By the end of this decade, $100 oil may seem like the good old days. And when you tell your children or grandchildren that you paid less than $3 a gallon for gasoline in 2005, it will seem as unbelievably inexpensive as a ten-cent chocolate bar or a ten-dollar suit.

The Case for Conservation

Doubtless, some will argue that as oil prices rise significantly higher, energy conservation will step in, lowering demand and bringing energy prices down again. Using history as a guide, we can estimate how high oil prices must go to trigger conservation, and how much energy it will save.

The longest and most powerful advance in oil prices during modern times occurred in the 1970s. So far, the recent gains in oil prices pale in comparison. In 1970 Saudi Arabian light oil, a good proxy for oil prices in general, averaged about $1.35 a barrel. The Arab oil embargo in 1973–74 and the consequent increase in OPEC's power translated into a nearly tenfold increase in oil prices over the next nine years. By 1979, that same oil, which traded for less than $1.50 a barrel in 1970, fetched over $13 a barrel. Then came the Iranian revolution, followed by the Iran-Iraq War. By 1982, light crude was trading for nearly $35 a barrel, or more than twenty-five times higher than in 1970.

A twenty-five-fold increase in twelve years works out to an annualized gain of about 30 percent a year. No bull market in any commodity or financial asset has maintained that high a growth rate for as long a time. Prices were so much higher near the end that they led to both conservation and the development of addi-

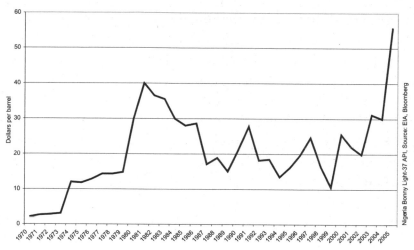

Crude Light Price

tional oil supplies and alternative energies. But first let us look at conservation.

In 1970, when oil traded at $1.35 a barrel, the world was consuming about 46 million barrels of oil a day (bpd). Though oil prices rose nearly ninefold over the next nine years, or at an annualized rate of about 29 percent, oil consumption continued to rise. By 1979, world consumption had grown to over 65 million bpd. In other words, the first tenfold increase in oil prices produced no conservation whatsoever. Now, consider that oil was trading near $10 a barrel in 1998. If history is any guide, oil will have to reach $100 a barrel before the world makes any significant effort at conservation.

But what if oil soared another 150 percent to the equivalent of $250 a barrel, an increase equivalent to that of the early 1980s? That might prompt conservation. Between 1979 and 1984, worldwide consumption of oil dropped from over 65 million bpd to about 59 million bpd, or nearly 10 percent. If we are optimistic, we might expect a similar degree of conservation this time around. Unfortunately, there is quite a bit more to the story.

During the early 1980s, as a result of energy conservation, the developed world experienced two recessions, a short one in 1980 and a much more protracted one in the 1981–82 period. In the United States, the highest quarterly GDP in 1980 was not exceeded until the beginning of 1983. Unemployment rose to over 10 percent. In other words, conservation came at a huge cost to the economy. As we will argue in the next chapter, a recession of that magnitude in today's world, with its historically high debt levels, would be potentially catastrophic. The government therefore will likely resist conservation for fear of the economic consequences.

Even assuming we were willing to endure 10 percent unemployment once again, would the world conserve to the same extent today as it did then? Would there be alternative energies available, as there were in the early 1980s—especially in the form of nuclear energy? We do not think so.

Although the world's consumption of oil did drop sharply between 1979 and 1984, worldwide economic growth during this period was particularly poor. Between 1979 and 1983, worldwide GDP growth averaged less than 2 percent a year, one of the weakest performances in postwar history.

More to the point, oil consumption decreased only in the developed world—in particular in the wealthier countries within the Organisation for Economic Co-operation and Development (OECD). These countries, which consist of Canada, France, Germany, Italy, Japan, Mexico, South Korea, Spain, the United Kingdom, and the United States, were responsible for all the conservation during that period.

Despite the weakened global economy, and an unprecedented surge in oil prices, oil consumption in developing countries, such as China and India, grew by nearly 5 percent in the period, or roughly 1 percent a year. And even within the OECD, South Korea, the least developed country, continued to increase its oil consumption.

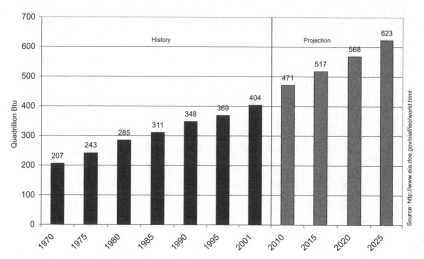

World Primary Energy Consumption

In today's world, as we have already pointed out, China and India are still developing economies in terms of per capita GDP and per capita consumption of virtually every commodity, including oil. Our conclusion is that even if oil reaches $260 a barrel, equivalent to the highs in the early 1980s, that might not be high enough to induce meaningful conservation in the world.

Almost by definition, a developing country needs oil to continue developing, to create economic growth. As noted in the August 22, 2005, issue of *Business Week*, "Both China and India need annual growth of at least 8% just to provide jobs for the tens of millions joining the workforce each year. Fear of worker unrest is a big reason Beijing has kept stoking its boom with massive lending and growth in the money supply."[14] For Chindia, growth is essential, and will require increasingly higher amounts of energy. Conservation would be a nightmare in China that could lead to massive unemployment and political revolution. Therefore, the Chinese government simply will not allow it.

---

14. Pete Engardio, "Crouching Tigers, Hidden Dragons," *Business Week*, August 22, 2005, 60–61.

Can We Not Increase Oil Production?

Of course, the preferred solution to the growing oil squeeze would be to increase our supply of oil and other forms of energy. This is what saved the economy in the early 1980s. When the Iran-Iraq War ended, Middle East oil could flow freely once more. Consequently, OPEC oil production climbed by 35 percent between the early 1980s and the end of the decade. Natural gas production, thanks to the lifting of price controls, also rose sharply. It went from about 18 percent of worldwide energy production to over 21 percent in the 1980s. As well, between 1980 and 1990, nuclear power generation more than doubled. By 1990, it provided 17 percent of the nation's electricity, compared with roughly 8 percent in 1980. These developments were much more important than conservation in checking the uptrend in oil prices.

Today, unfortunately, so few believe oil prices are in a protracted uptrend that there are no meaningful alternative energies waiting in the wings. (As we will show in a later chapter, the most viable alternative, wind, has received only token support.) Moreover, the fault for this is society's shortsighted—if not completely blind—mind-set toward the future, a shortsightedness that can only be explained by groupthink and the wrenching experiments of Milgram and Asch.

Nor, as was the case in the 1980s, are there meaningful amounts of additional hydrocarbons waiting to come onstream. Worldwide oil exploration has suffered from declining returns for some time, despite the use of improved technology. It has been decades since the last giant oil reservoirs were discovered, and even large discoveries are becoming rarer. Let us quote an excellent description of the dilemma written by James J. MacKenzie in *Issues in Science and Technology* (June 22, 1996):

> According to the U.S. Geological Survey (USGS), global discovery of large new oil fields peaked in 1962 and has been declining since. The reason is simple: Most oil occurs

in a few very large oil fields and these are usually discovered early on because they are so big. The largest 1 percent of oil fields contain 75 percent of all the discovered oil, and the largest 3 percent contain 94 percent of the oil. The implication of this skewed distribution is that as exploration progresses, the average size of the fields discovered decreases. In other words, exploration in the declining phase of oil development—where we find ourselves today—is a far different game than in the early phase. In the early stages, it is the large fields that are readily discovered; in the declining stages, geologists are much more likely to find small fields and oil companies must do a lot more drilling just to stay even. That's why it's so much harder to maintain production in the declining stages than in the growing phase of the industry.

In other words, we can safely assume that virtually all significant oil deposits in the planet's crust have already been found. Further exploration will result in ever smaller discoveries, and an ever higher exploration cost per barrel of oil discovered.

Once again, the world must turn to the Middle East, specifically Saudi Arabia, as the only possible source of additional oil production. However, there is another problem that is generally overlooked.

The Problem with Other People's Oil

Let us assume that the Saudis' oil reserves are as large as they claim—which, as we have mentioned, is not entirely certain. It takes energy to produce energy—a lot of it. Saudi Arabia is a relatively small country with about 20 million residents. Of the roughly 10 million bpd of oil Saudi Arabia currently produces, it consumes some 2 million bpd, or 20 percent. Despite its oil riches, the country has experienced very little per capita GDP growth over the past decade. However, in the past, when it has experienced strong economic growth, its internal demand for energy grew at a double-digit rate.

If we accept the heroic and undoubtedly unrealistic claim by the Department of Energy that the Saudis will double their oil production from 10 to 20 million bpd over the next fifteen years, clearly such a project will require huge chunks of capital, which will provide a considerable boost to Saudi Arabia's economic growth.

So it is safe to assume that the Saudis' own energy consumption will again grow by about 10 percent a year. This implies that by the time Saudi Arabia reaches a production level of 20 million bpd, its internal oil consumption will have increased to about 8 million bpd (6 million bpd more than they are currently using). In other words, they will end up consuming more than half of their new oil production themselves.

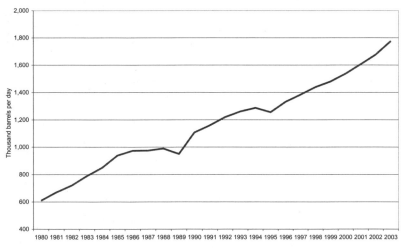

Saudi Arabian Petroleum Consumption

Some, such as Edward Morse and James Richard, whom we cited in chapter 2, have argued that Russia will also be a major contributor of new oil production. Here is one more quote from their 2002 article: "In the long term, Moscow may have far more going for it than Riyadh. Yukos, Lukoil, are dynamic and growing."

Russia did look promising, for a time. Between 1995 and 1998 Russian oil production hovered around 6 million bpd. Then, beginning in 1999, Russian oil production began to accelerate, rising to over 11 million bpd in 2004. This huge increase represented about 70 percent of the gain in non-OPEC production during that period. So yes, between 1999 and 2004 Russia was a very big deal.

However, in 2005 Russian oil production barely increased at all. In addition, Yukos has not only lost its dynamism but has ceased to exist as Russia has reverted ever closer to a totalitarian form of government.

In fact, it is no coincidence that the rise and fall of Russia as a critical contributor to oil production growth coincided almost exactly with the fortunes of Yukos. Yukos began as a public company in the late 1990s. In early 1999, its stock was worth about 10 rubles per share. By 2003–4, the stock was trading at between 300 and 500 rubles. And then the bottom fell out. The chairman of Yukos was arrested and the company was effectively taken over by the state. With the demise of Yukos, capitalism died in Russia, and very likely so did its future as a major oil producer.

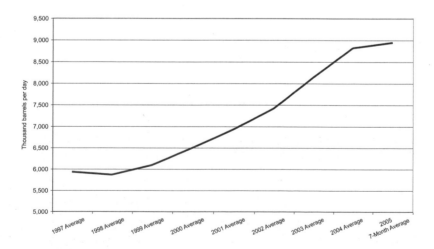

Russian Crude Oil Production

But there is more than politics involved. As with Saudi Arabia, there is the issue of Russia's internal need for oil. When the Soviet Union collapsed in the early 1990s, Russia experienced a hideous depression, so hideous that life expectancy fell sharply. Energy consumption fell dramatically for a time, as did energy production. Eventually, energy production recovered and began outpacing energy consumption, largely because of the creation of Yukos and other oil companies. But had Russian oil consumption since 1990 remained consistent with the cold war era—growing by one or two percentage points a year—then even with resurgent energy production in the early 2000s, Russia would have had virtually no energy to export today.

Clearly, if Russia tries to become a stronger exporter of oil and other minerals, its own economy is going to grow rapidly. And that will mean a much greater internal need for energy.

It is no accident that the vast majority of oil exports come from countries with immature economies and weak political structures. Countries that are rapidly growing eventually need all the energy they produce and then some for their own internal needs. Another example is Iran, which is perhaps the fastest-growing OPEC nation and the second-largest exporter of oil. One reason Iran claims it needs nuclear reactors is that within a decade it will be a net importer of energy. If so, from where will Iran get the oil it needs?

So How High Could Oil Go?

In chapter 2, we mentioned the concept of Hubbert's law, which is alternatively referred to by the term "Hubbert's Peak," the point in time at which global oil production enters a permanent decline. Many writers, including Colin Campbell and Kenneth Deffeyes, argue that the world has already passed or is within just a few years of passing Hubbert's Peak. In other words, oil production will soon be unable to meet any increase in demand.

Although there is nothing facile about these arguments, our view is that even without them there is more than enough evidence for us to believe a crisis of epic proportions is brewing. Everything points toward an energy crisis that will be at least as severe as the one the United States experienced in the 1970s.

As we mentioned earlier, between 1970 and 1982, oil prices went from $1.35 a barrel to a high of nearly $35. That is a twenty-six-fold increase. To match that experience this decade, the price of oil would have to reach $260 a barrel.

Of course, history seldom repeats itself with perfect accuracy. In the 1970s, the oil crisis was primarily political. This time around, the issue is a ceiling on supply—a more difficult problem to solve.

We therefore do not want to declare $260 a precise target for oil. All we can say is that oil prices will reach a very painful level, one that will likely threaten the very fabric of our economy and society—indeed the world's economy.

If we did not think there was a chance of getting through, we would not be writing this book in the first place. Nonetheless, it is important to realize just how challenging the coming years could be. So, with that in mind, we will now consider what a world with $200-plus oil will look like.

CHAPTER 8

The Havoc That Will Result from $200 Oil

A world in which oil prices climb relentlessly higher will challenge civilization's leaders more severely than any other crisis in living memory—more than even the Great Depression and World War II. The rapidly approaching oil shortage may be the greatest test of civilization and the world economy since the advent of the Industrial Revolution. In fact, unless our leaders act quickly and aggressively, our chances of surviving as a complex society are rather low.

Using past energy crises as a guide, we can deduce some of the challenges the looming crisis will bring. But let us be clear from the outset: the effects of the oil supply shortfall we will face over the next few years will be more severe than those of any previous energy crisis, particularly because the coming crisis will be *permanent*. We have little hope that oil production can continue rising to a meaningful degree. Most likely, it will enter a gradual decline. The only thing that could slow demand for oil would be a global recession, and even that would only be temporary. Clearly, the world of the future will be one in which oil grows ever more costly.

Government policymakers will find the next ten years or so especially frustrating, for the following reasons.

Inflation, Deflation, and the Policymakers' Dilemma

In a world of runaway oil prices, none of the old rules will apply. Two-hundred-dollar oil will challenge the government's ability to manage the economy through fiscal and monetary policy. By fiscal and monetary policy, we mean spending, interest rates, financial liquidity, and the other tools the federal government and the Federal Reserve Bank use to regulate economic growth.

In what is accepted as the "normal" scheme of things, the economy oscillates between periods of inflation and deflation, or between growth and recession. The government tries to reduce the volatility or amplitude of these cycles, to prevent the hardship caused by extreme swings. For example, we noted in chapter 6 that our government learned, through the experience of the Great Depression and similar events, that the way to deal with an economic slowdown is to stimulate growth with a fast infusion of cash. The federal government can deliver cash infusions by lowering interest rates, increasing spending, or lowering taxes. Correspondingly, when the economy grows too quickly, causing inflation, the government will respond by raising interest rates, raising taxes, and decreasing government spending. Making less money available by these methods puts the brakes on economic growth.

The problem with rising energy costs is that they are both inflationary and deflationary at the same time, which makes it difficult for the government to choose the right strategy.

First, consider how rising oil prices add to inflation. Historically, energy has become the driving force behind inflation whenever energy expenditures reached 10 percent of GDP. That was the case in the 1970s, the last time the inflation rate rose to double digits. Energy costs peaked at about 13 percent of economic activity during the 1980–81 period, a time in which inflation by many measures was 15 percent and higher. In fact, even at

8 percent of GDP, as in 1973–75, energy costs contribute significantly to inflation.

For an analogy of how rising energy costs add to inflation, consider gasoline, a product whose price affects us all. The price of gasoline is made up of the price of oil, plus the price of refining, shipping, labor, and other costs to bring it to the pump.

For simplicity's sake, let us say, hypothetically, that at one time gasoline cost $1 a gallon. We will also assume that the cost of oil made up 20 percent of the price of gasoline, and all the other costs made up the remaining 80 percent. In the last chapter, we looked at what happens when one component of the world economy grows faster than the rest. Now we can apply the same reasoning to the cost of goods. If the price of oil doubles each year, while the other costs stay fixed, we get the following results:

Year	Oil	Other costs	Gasoline	Increase
0	$0.20	$0.80	$1.00	0% (base case)
1	$0.40	$0.80	$1.20	20%
2	$0.80	$0.80	$1.60	33%
3	$1.60	$0.80	$2.40	50%
4	$3.20	$0.80	$4.00	67%
5	$6.40	$0.80	$7.20	80%

As you can see, each time the price of oil doubles, it has a bigger effect on the price of gasoline. The longer this trend continues, the more important the price of oil becomes. Eventually, every increase in oil will produce an almost equal increase in gasoline prices. All other costs will be almost irrelevant.

Since its 1998 low, the price of oil has increased more than sixfold. Meanwhile, mercifully, the price of gasoline in America has only risen 2.5-fold. So gasoline prices have trailed behind oil prices. But the higher oil prices get, the closer the relationship between oil and gas becomes. When oil went from $20 to $28 (a 40 percent gain), it had very little effect on the price of gas. But with oil over $60 in 2005, gasoline prices were markedly higher— over $3 a gallon in some areas. So the higher oil prices get, the bigger the increase in the price of fuels.

Of course, gasoline is just one product that rising oil prices will affect. Apart from transportation fuel, oil is used for home heating. It is a raw material for making plastics, asphalt, and a host of other chemical products. Oil is used to make fertilizer for food production and to run farm equipment. And of course, oil provides the energy for manufacturing virtually every product consumers buy. Higher fuel costs also mean higher costs for shipping those products, particularly today when so many products are manufactured overseas. So as time goes on, rising oil prices will mean accelerating costs for almost everything, which is of course the definition of runaway inflation.

In 2001, energy costs accounted for nearly 7 percent of GDP. Unfortunately, due to multiyear lag times in assembling the data, the Energy Information Administration has yet to release more recent figures. However, some analysts expect energy spending to reach 8.7 percent of GDP in 2005. In addition, oil prices since 2001 have gone from $30 a barrel to over $60. So it is safe to assume that energy prices are again becoming a significant part of economic activity, and the climb toward double-digit inflation may have already begun. The more expensive oil becomes, the faster inflation will rise.

Just in case you think double-digit inflation is an outlandish prediction, consider that in less than a century this country has already experienced three bouts of it. These were during the First World War, the Second World War, and the 1970–82 period. Just like today, all three bouts were characterized by massive government deficits and resource shortages.

Another side effect of energy crises and inflation is higher unemployment. Rising prices cause workers to demand higher wages, which in turn discourages employers from hiring. Usually, this effect is unnoticed, since inflation occurs at the same time as economic growth. Growth tends to create new jobs, offsetting inflation's negative effect on employment. However, the situation is radically different when inflation is driven by rising energy prices. An energy squeeze tends to suppress economic growth at the same time as it adds to inflation, so that unemployment becomes noticeably higher.

This is why we say spiraling oil prices are deflationary as well as inflationary. They are deflationary because when individuals and businesses must pay more for oil, they have less money to spend on other products and services, resulting in lower economic growth and higher unemployment. Because the United States is an importer of oil, money spent on oil emigrates to oil-producing nations, thus worsening the trade deficit. Oil-producing nations enjoy higher income as oil prices rise, which gives a boost to their GDP. However, that boost is traditionally not enough to offset the GDP loss within importing countries, so the overall global economy weakens.[15]

In one sense, rising oil prices are like taxes. They add to the cost of everything, while discouraging business expansion. In another sense, they are worse than taxes, because taxes at least promote a balanced government budget. While tax revenues can finance social programs, or other stimulative government spending, oil expenditures cannot. If we recall that high taxes were partly to blame for the fall of the Roman Empire, we can easily imagine how high oil prices could contribute to the fall of our civilization. Oil prices of over $200 a barrel will increase the cost of maintaining a complex society—and simultaneously lower the rewards. As we have pointed out, declining returns from complexity have contributed to the fall of many past civilizations.

In the energy crises of the 1970s, the inflationary/deflationary effects of rising energy costs led to stagflation—a combination of

---

15. Valeria Costantini and Francesco Gracceva, "Social Costs of Energy Disruptions," *Nota di Lavoro* 116 (September 2004).

high unemployment, high inflation, and economic recession. In 1970, unemployment was less than 5 percent, but it rose steadily throughout the 1970s until it finally peaked during 1982–83 at over 10 percent. We were lucky the crisis did not last, and that energy supplies increased. Otherwise, unemployment might have risen to the level where it provoked widespread social unrest.

Nonetheless, we can see the bind in which government policymakers will soon find themselves. Following the technology crash, monetary policy went into stimulation mode—boosting liquidity, lowering taxes, and lowering interest rates. Spending money on military campaigns was also a positive factor, since government spending promotes growth. As oil prices rise, stifling growth, policymakers will want to maintain their stimulative stance. However, as energy prices rise, so will inflation. As citizens find their monthly bills increasing, policymakers will feel pressured to deal with inflation and stimulate growth at the same time.

To make matters worse, government spending will likely increase over the coming decade. The oldest members of the baby boomer generation will reach age sixty-five by 2010. As they retire, government spending on Social Security, Medicare, and other social programs will rise dramatically. As the energy crisis worsens, and with continued unrest in the Middle East, the U.S. government will likely need to increase military spending to protect America's access to the largest remaining oil reserves. As well, we sincerely hope our society begins a serious campaign to develop alternative energy sources that can reduce our dependence on oil. Such an effort will be essential if civilization as we know it is to survive, but it will come with a hefty price tag—as high as $1 trillion, by some estimates.

As we mentioned above, government spending has a stimulative effect on the economy. It increases both growth and inflation. In the ten years preceding each of the most recent periods of double-digit inflation (World War I, World War II, and the late 1960s to early 1980s), government spending tripled. Likewise, we expect higher government spending will add to inflationary pressures over the coming decade and beyond.

Policymakers will then have to choose between two options. They could fight inflation by choking growth and running the risk of recession, or they could stimulate growth and allow inflation to reach double digits.

When this dilemma arose in the late 1970s and early 1980s, the government decided that inflation was the worse of the two evils. Paul Volcker, Federal Reserve chairman, decided to bring inflation under control by curtailing growth. He engineered a recession by raising interest rates far above the level of inflation. That recession, balanced with energy conservation and new energy supplies in the form of nuclear power and additional oil capacity, brought inflation under control without destroying the economy.

When soaring oil prices lead to the rebirth of stagflation (the most likely scenario for the next decade), we cannot say which policy the government will choose. However, we doubt Volcker's solution will be repeated. In the first place, no new energy supplies are waiting to come online this time. The energy crisis stems from supply/demand fundamentals, not politics. That increases the risk that higher interest rates could trigger a severe recession—another depression, in fact. If the Great Depression taught us anything, it taught us that severe recession and deflation are no trifling problems. That alone will make policymakers cautious about raising interest rates.

However, there is another reason why sky-high interest rates are not an option this time around.

Hindered by Debt

In the 1980s, we had the luxury of a relatively unleveraged economy. That is no longer the case. Today's economy is far more burdened by debt than it has ever been. Not only is government debt at record highs ($7.8 trillion at last count), but every measure of consumer debt is far greater than in the 1980s. For example, today mortgage debt represents about 50 percent of home equity, while in the late 1970s and early 1980s the figure was about 40 percent. The value of real estate loans at commercial banks alone has doubled since 1999. In addition, over 70 percent of a record amount of consumer lending today is secured by homes.

As inflation rises rapidly over the next few years, our nation's high debt levels will effectively prevent policymakers from applying the same medicine that Volcker used in the 1980s. The Federal Reserve knows that if it were to raise interest rates dramatically in order to slow the economy, it would risk a major collapse in home prices—something far worse than even double-digit inflation.

Never in postwar history have home prices suffered a collapse. Home prices in nominal terms have risen throughout every recession since 1950. Moreover, the fact that home prices rose during the early 2000s probably saved the economy from far greater harm. No wonder then that consumers have put so much faith in their homes. No wonder they are willing to use their homes to secure borrowing.

However, if home prices suddenly started to fall, the result would easily be the vicious circle to end all vicious circles. In mid-1981, the Federal Reserve raised interest rates to more than five percentage points above the inflation rate. That made interest rates much higher than the rate at which investors could reasonably expect homes or any other asset to increase.

If the Fed applied that same tactic today, not only would borrowing on homes cease, but consumers would be scrambling to come up with mortgage payments. In the case of adjustable rate mortgages, payments would be rising rapidly. At the same time, demand for homes would fall dramatically. After all, one reason for buying a home is that you expect its price will rise at least in line with inflation. However, that would not be the case if interest rates on home mortgages were much higher than inflation. With mortgages such a large portion of home values, many homeowners would doubtless be forced to sell their homes. Home prices would tumble further, and the resulting downward spiral could easily be curtains for the economy.

Consider the technology bubble for a moment. In 2000, stocks represented more wealth than homes. So you might assume that if we survived a major decline in stock prices, we could survive a similar decline in home prices. Unfortunately, survival would not be so easy with home prices falling. Declining home prices would also mean a slumping economy and slumping stocks as a result. In the early 2000s, the Fed was able to support home prices and consumer spending by sharply lowering interest rates. Stocks, though admittedly they were the biggest chunk of economic wealth, were still concentrated in a relatively small portion of the economy. Home values are a bigger deal because far more people own homes than own stocks, and the average person has more wealth tied up in his or her home than in the stock market.

With home prices, stock prices, and the economy all slumping, all feeding on one another, it would indeed be a vicious circle. Record levels of unemployment would be likely. Could the policymakers rescue such a situation? Clearly, it would be a far greater challenge than rescuing the economy in the wake of the tech bubble. It would take massive amounts of money. Interest rates would likely fall to zero. Government spending would need to reach unimaginably high levels. In other words, if the economy survived, it would emerge with much higher debt levels than before. Moreover, we would still face the same hideous inflationary problem, a shortage of energy, and the prospect of sharply rising oil prices.

Admittedly, during such a recession, oil prices would likely decline, at least temporarily. However, the fallout could even be worse than we have described—much worse. After all, we are only talking about the U.S. economy. What would happen in the developing world, namely China and India, if the United States went through a massive economic contraction? It is impossible to say, but if the Chinese economy were to collapse, leading to widespread social unrest there and in other parts of the world, then rescuing the U.S. economy, which is so interdependent with the rest of the world, would be that much harder.

The bottom line is that fighting inflation would be economic suicide in a world where oil prices are racing past the $200 mark. Moreover, allowing millions of Americans to lose their homes would spell political suicide for the governing party, not to mention create massive social problems due to higher numbers of homeless persons. Therefore, fighting inflation is out of the question.

The Only Imaginable Solution

Unable to fight inflation without risking an economic meltdown, from which our society might never recover, policymakers will put all their efforts into keeping the economy growing, so that wages rise faster than interest rates and debt does not overwhelm the average citizen. They will have no option but to allow inflation to reach heights that would have been considered unacceptable in any previous decade.

Inflation will also seem more appealing than depression because it will reduce the degree to which the economy is held hostage to debt. As inflation further lifts the prices of homes and other assets, it will diminish the weight of the debt underlying those assets. For instance, if you own a home worth $1 million, and you have a $1 million mortgage, your debt burden is almost unbearable. In effect, you own nothing. However, if inflation causes your home to be worth $2 million and doubles your income, your debt will become much more manageable.

The government will find that the same thing is true about its own debts. It will be much easier to pay them off with dollars that are worth less, thanks to inflation.

Even if policymakers were crazy enough to try to fight inflation, and we were lucky enough to survive, it would still only postpone the day of reckoning. We would come out of that severe recession with an even more leveraged economy, a much shakier world economy, and no change in the chronic shortage of oil. Even though oil prices would have dipped during the recession, a growing world would quickly eat up all the slack in oil and then some. The same cycle would repeat—but even more violently.

So the real question is not whether inflation will rise, but how high it will go and at what point it might threaten the very fabric of our society. Unfortunately, there is no way of saying where the threshold lies. History is replete with instances in which ultra-high inflation has destroyed societies. The hyperinflation of the 1920s in Germany destroyed the middle class in that country and gave birth to Hitler. Hyperinflation, by the loosest definition, means a cumulative three-year increase in the consumer price index (CPI) of over 100 percent. However, it will not take such extremes to create financial hardship across America.

The battle royal over the next decade will clearly be between the destructive forces of inflation and depression. With oil moving toward $200 a barrel and higher, the risk of economic collapse will be greater than at any time in the history of capitalism. This is not to say civilization must fall. In later chapters, we will outline the choices society has open to it. We will even suggest our preferred course of action.

Nonetheless, time is not on our side. Our society has ignored the problem of a fixed ceiling on oil production for decades. Now that the crisis is on our doorstep, we doubt even the best possible course of action can prevent years of hardship. However, if we want our civilization to survive, and to emerge at the end of the next decade in a stronger position than before, then our leaders must now begin to acknowledge the problem. They must free themselves from the closed-minded errors of groupthink, see the growing oil shortage for what it is, and create a long-term plan for our survival.

CHAPTER 9

What the 1970s Teach Us About Investing in the Coming Decade

I f the coming decade will be challenging for government policy-makers, it will be even more so for individual investors. We cannot say how challenging, since we have never faced an oil crisis of such severity. What we can say is that the investment climate will look nothing like that of the 1990s for a long time to come.

The bull market of the 1990s was one of the most exciting times in history to be an investor. It was probably the easiest time to make money in stocks since the 1920s. It has been said that, at the height of the 1920s bull market, you could throw a dart at the list of stocks trading on the New York Exchange, and whatever stock you hit would almost certainly go up. The same seemed to be true about technology and e-commerce stocks in the late 1990s.

The 1990s was also a special period because the number of investors increased dramatically. Before then, only a small percentage of the population owned stocks—generally those with a high income or inherited savings. But as the baby boomer generation entered their peak retirement savings years, more money began flowing into retirement savings plans and 401(k)s. Books such as

Wealth Without Risk and *The Wealthy Barber* explained how easy it would be for even an average wage earner to amass a million-dollar nest egg by the time he or she retired, simply by investing in equity mutual funds. All it took was a regular savings plan, and perhaps a little dollar-cost averaging, and the magic of compound returns would do the rest. Consequently, the number of American households that owned shares in mutual funds rose from 5.7 percent in 1980 to a high of 49.6 percent in 2002.

All this new money pouring into equity funds naturally helped drive stock prices higher. In a reflexive manner, the resulting bull market proved the theory that anyone could become rich through equities. Good returns drew more money into equity funds, and money flowing into equities supported the bull market. Consequently, more people made a point of learning about investments, and gained the courage to trade stocks directly.

As a result of the 1990s bull market, millions of investors today have very high expectations about what returns their investments should generate. The technology crash may have dashed a few hopes, but many investors still cling to the beliefs and strategies they acquired during the bull market of the 1990s. In their shortsighted view, the 1990s was the "normal" state of affairs, which they expect—and in many cases desperately hope—will soon return.

However, we must point out that the bull market of the 1990s, particularly the late 1990s, was far from typical—if there is such a thing as a typical decade in the markets. The 1990s was also a period in which inflation and oil prices were relatively low and stable. Because energy is a crucial determinant of investment performance, we doubt the coming decade will resemble the 1990s in any way, shape, or form. While we cannot say exactly what the future will be like, we suspect today's growing oil crisis will make investment returns over the next ten years look much more like those of the 1970s, a period when the United States endured two energy crises in less than eight years and inflation reached double digits. In other words, while some investors will grow incredibly wealthy (and yes, we will explain how you can be one of those people), the majority will experience a great deal of disappointment.

A More Likely Scenario

Anyone who was born after 1970 will have only a dim recollection what living through the energy crises of the 1970s was like. Most of the adults at that time had grown up in an era when oil was so cheap and abundant it could be taken for granted. Consequently, the huge gains in energy prices in the 1970s, accompanied by occasional shortages, were emotionally traumatic as well as financially painful.

After World War II, American cities had been built with the assumption that cars would always be widely owned and gasoline would remain inexpensive, so suburbs became the norm. That was the shortsighted groupthink at the time, which failed to recognize that one day oil production would decline and transportation fuel would become more costly. Consequently, when gasoline prices began to soar they had a major impact on the average citizen's lifestyle.

As a result of the energy crises of 1973–74 and 1979, oil went from under $3 a barrel to over $35, prompting the government to experiment with a whole slew of emergency conservation measures. In 1973, the Emergency Petroleum Allocation Act put controls on the production, marketing, and price of gasoline that resulted in long lines at service stations. For a time, if your car had even-numbered license plates, you could buy gasoline only on even-numbered days. If your car had odd-numbered license plates, you could buy gas only on odd-numbered days. Schools and offices sometimes closed to save heating oil. Factories reduced production and laid off workers. The government tried imposing year-round daylight savings time and a national speed limit of 55 mph. Higher gasoline prices forced automakers to start building smaller cars, and to increase fuel efficiency by incorporating features such as front-wheel drive. President Carter installed solar panels and a woodstove at the White House, and money became available for research into wind and solar energy.

Of course, later governments rescinded many of these policies after the energy crises ended. President Reagan, for example, had the solar panels removed from the White House. Nonetheless, we expect to see a new drive toward energy conservation and alternative energy development within the next ten years, once most people realize oil prices are in a permanent uptrend.

The 1970s were also an era of rising inflation. Since 1991, inflation has remained below 4 percent a year, which means many of today's investors have little experience living in a high-inflation environment. Those who are older will remember the incredible hardship and anxiety people endured in the 1970s.

When the price of the most mundane items in the grocery store rose each week, for months on end, while paychecks mostly stayed the same, many people began to fear for their future. They postponed new purchases because they could not be certain of keeping up with the payments. Those who had children grew especially anxious. And those who were retired, or otherwise living on a fixed income, suffered the worst anxiety of all. They had no chance of increasing their income, so their lifestyle could only go down. Millions of average people looked at their monthly bills and wondered at what point they would have to choose between food and rent. In the early 1980s, after a decade of rising inflation, homelessness became a major social issue.

To take a minor example, today you can expect to pay millions of dollars for a co-op apartment on Park Avenue in New York City. During the worst period in the 1970s, some of these apartments were being practically given away to anyone who could afford to pay the maintenance fees. If gasoline costs over $3 a gallon in your neighborhood today, all we can tell you is, you haven't seen anything yet!

When prices are rising rapidly, businesses cannot estimate future costs or the value of future inventories. They become reluctant to launch new enterprises or take on new employees. Consequently, the high inflation of the 1970s caused unemployment to rise until it peaked at over 10 percent in 1982. Economists in the 1970s created the "Misery Index," the sum of the inflation rate and the unemployment rate, to measure how unhappy the American public's situation was becoming.

Investing in a High-Inflation/ High-Energy-Price Era

The 1970s also stand out as being both the best of times and the worst of times for investors. It was the best of times for a handful of independent thinkers who recognized where the real opportunities lay and were courageous enough to capitalize on them. It was the worst of times for the vast majority.

What made the 1970s painful for most investors was the high inflation rate. Inflation destroys wealth because it causes the dollars to be worth less over time (as measured in purchasing power). If your annual investment returns are less than the inflation rate, you may have more dollars, but in fact you are becoming poorer.

Inflation destroys a person's wealth far more effectively than even deflation. Deflation, such as we had in the Great Depression, can destroy an economy, but at least individuals can preserve their wealth by trading in their investments for cash. During deflation, prices fall, making cash worth more. So you can actually increase the buying power of your savings by converting your assets into cash until the deflationary period has ended.

However, high inflation destroys the value of all investments—cash included—making it much harder to preserve, let alone grow, wealth. In the 1970s, the average annual inflation rate was higher than the yield on cash or bonds, so that the real return (returns minus inflation) on cash was –1.1 percent a year, and the real return on bonds was –1.9 percent. Because cash and bonds are traditionally considered safer investments than stocks, they are widely held by senior citizens, pension funds, and other investors who need income but cannot afford capital losses. Inflation therefore resulted in devastating losses for those who were least able to withstand them.

In the coming energy crisis, the devastation will likely be worse than in the 1970s. Because the energy shortage will be more severe and permanent, inflation may rise much higher and faster.

On top of that, the demographics have changed. In 1975, members of the baby boomer generation were still young— between ten and thirty years old. Even the ones who had begun their careers had decades ahead of them to save for retirement. By the time most of them became serious about investing, inflation was already falling. In the 1990s, when the baby boomers were in their peak saving and investing years, inflation was low and stable. Consequently, the boomers have never needed to worry much about it. They see high inflation as a historic problem that affected their parents, but was solved long ago.

Today, however, the baby boomers are nearing retirement. They constitute 76 million people—the largest generation in America— who will soon need to shift their money into a safe haven where it will fund their retirement. Every well-trained financial adviser will be telling them to invest a good portion of their money in safe assets like bonds and money market instruments (i.e., cash). When soaring energy prices drive up inflation, the resulting losses and hardship could far exceed what happened in their parents' generation.

The other obvious difference between the 1970s and the 1990s is that in the 1970s the stock markets were much more volatile. Between 1982 and 1999, stocks underwent only two bear markets, both of which were exceptionally brief and painless. For example, despite the bear market in 1987, which culminated in the famous Black Monday crash on October 19, stocks still finished the year in positive territory. Moreover, in the other bear market, 1990–91, only minimal losses occurred. This is why by the late 1990s it had become "common knowledge" or groupthink that stocks "always go up," at least among the shortsighted investors who make up the majority. Only those with a longer sense of history remembered that stocks can also fall—sometimes a lot farther and for a lot longer than most investors can bear.

For example, between 1966 and 1982, stocks underwent six bear markets in which prices fell by 20 percent or more. In between, of course, were bull markets when stock prices rose. Such zigzagging volatility was the natural result of the uncertainty caused by rising inflation and energy prices.

As oil prices climb over the next few years, driving inflation higher, we would not be surprised to see stocks exhibit volatility equal or greater than that of the 1970s. Uncertainty will reign once again.

Fortunately, the bear markets should not be too severe. As we explained in the last chapter, economic growth has become an absolute necessity in today's leveraged, high-debt world. Just as an individual with a lot of debt cannot tolerate a significant drop in income, a debt-heavy economy cannot tolerate a slowdown in growth. Federal policymakers know this and will feel obliged to maintain a stimulative stance to encourage economic growth. As a consequence, rising profits will protect stocks from an outright collapse.

Unfortunately, just as in the 1970s, the bull markets in coming years will also be limited by the higher inflation that will result from rising oil prices, economic growth, and higher government spending. In the 1970s, profits among S&P 500 stocks grew at an annualized rate of 11 percent, roughly twice the historical aver-

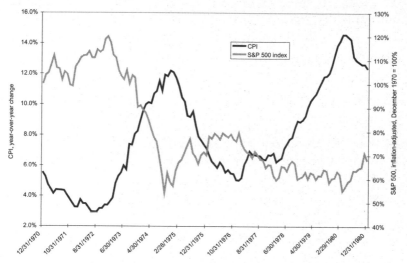

Consumer Price Index (CPI) and S&P 500 (Inflation-Adjusted) in the 1970s

age. However, much of that growth simply reflected rising inflation. Profits generated by inflation are worth less than profits from actual business expansion, and so investors value them less highly. As a result, price/earnings ratios dropped dramatically in the 1970s. The combination of rising earnings and falling P/Es kept stock prices confined within a broad trading range, which centered around 100 on the S&P 500.

A trading range—a sideways, zigzag pattern similar to what occurred in the 1970s—is the most likely scenario for the coming years. Certainly, it is much more likely than a renewed, long-term bull market. However, a trading range does not mean flat returns for investors. If stocks tread water while inflation is rising, real returns will actually be falling.

In real terms, the 1970s was the worst decade ever for stocks, at least for the majority of investors. As you can see from the following table, it was the only decade since 1930 in which stocks lost money in real terms.

S&P 500 Performance

Decade	Annualized real return	Total real return
1930s	2.0%	21.9%
1940s	3.8%	45.2%
1950s	17.2%	389.0%
1960s	5.3%	67.6%
1970s	−1.5%	−14.0%
1980s	12.5%	124.7%
1990s	15.3%	315.2%

Even during the Great Depression, from 1929 to 1944, the real return on stocks averaged 1.5 percent a year. If you had invested in the S&P 500 in 1929, you would have made 25 percent in real terms by the end. On the other hand, between 1966 and 1981, while the S&P 500 produced an average annual gain of 6 percent, inflation averaged 7 percent a year. So in real terms, a buy-and-hold investor would have lost 14 percent over the period.

Unrealistic Expectations

We noted above that, for a few investors, the 1970s were the best of times. And so they were. Nevertheless, making money in a high-inflation/high-energy-price environment is much more difficult than it was in the 1990s. In fact, many of the approaches to investing that became popular and had good results in the 1990s are likely to lead to losses over the next few years. Investors who want to make real returns must therefore adopt a new approach as quickly as possible.

For example, in the 1990s investors came to believe almost universally that diversification leads to higher, safer gains. The safest way to make money, if you were a passive or novice investor, was to buy a well-diversified mutual fund, or perhaps an index fund, that tracked the performance of the S&P 500. In the 1970s, nothing was further from the truth. When real returns are negative, tracking the broad market will only make you poorer. The investors who made solid returns in the 1970s were those who shunned diversification and concentrated their holdings in those few sectors and stocks whose returns exceeded inflation.

One of the most surprising things about the 1970s was that good companies with solid growth—the kind that get high marks from analysts—often delivered poor returns. For example, consider the nation's leading retailer back in the 1970s, Kmart. In 1970, Kmart's P/E ratio was in the mid-20s. Throughout the 1970s, Kmart's earnings grew at a compound annualized rate of nearly 17 percent—a solid performance. Yet due to high inflation, Kmart's P/E ratio dropped into single digits by the end of the 1970s. Its annualized return, including dividends, was only about 2 percent a year. With inflation rising by an average of 7 percent a year, investors in Kmart actually lost 5 percent a year in real terms.

The lesson is that, unlike the 1990s, in a high-inflation climate, investors cannot be satisfied with growth that is merely good. Nor can they gain any safety from tracking the broad market. To beat inflation, they need to focus their investment capital on stocks whose earnings growth is exceptional.

In the 1970s, the strongest growth occurred among companies whose market capitalization was under $1 billion—the small-cap stocks. Small-cap stocks had an advantage because they started with a smaller revenue and earnings base. It was therefore much easier for small-cap companies to increase their income than large-cap companies, and that fact helped them overcome the downward pressure on P/E ratios.

Naturally, as oil prices rose in the 1970s, one of the best sectors to be in was oil stocks. The gains from oil stocks were more than double those of the S&P 500. Oil service companies in particular enjoyed average annual gains of 31 percent. Another sector that did very well in the 1970s was gold, for the simple reason that gold tends to rise along with inflation. During the 1970s, the

S&P gold stock index climbed at an annualized rate of 37.5 percent. Gold itself hit an all-time high of over $800 an ounce in 1980.

The fact that gold and oil have produced solid gains in the past few years is yet another sign that the current climate is becoming increasingly like the 1970s. We would not be surprised to see these sectors continue to outperform as the energy crisis unfolds. Since current groupthink says oil prices will average $30–$50 a barrel long-term, many oil stocks today are greatly undervalued compared to what their assets will be worth once the financial world realizes oil is on its way to three figures. Similarly, gold currently suffers from a prevailing negative bias among investors, because it languished in the low-inflation environment of the 1990s, when so many of today's investors cut their teeth. Today, most investors have little regard for it. Consequently, gold and gold stocks are also undervalued compared to their long-term potential.

Another 1990s-style strategy investors must dispense with is buying and holding stocks or mutual funds for the long term. In the long bull market of the 1990s, "buy and hold" worked wonders for millions of passive investors who just rode the market up. If an investor is many decades away from retirement, most financial advisers will still recommend against selling stocks, even during a bear market. The theory is that investors will make up any losses they incur when the next big bull market comes around.

However, buy and hold was a very disappointing strategy in the volatile market of the 1970s. As the market zigged and zagged, any gains buy-and-holders made in a bull phase were wiped out in the next bear phase or else consumed by inflation. Given the choice, most investors prefer not to lose money in any decade, and retired persons especially cannot wait twenty years to make back their losses. Therefore, a far more rewarding strategy in the 1970s was to sell shares at the market tops and buy them again at the start of the next rally.

To summarize, making money in the 1970s took a lot more effort than in the 1990s. Rather than simply buy a diversified portfolio, sit back, and watch it grow, successful investors in the 1970s had to actively scout out the most undervalued and fastest-growing sectors and companies, study the market trends, and be ready to jump in and out of stocks at the right moments.

As the current energy squeeze intensifies, the market climate will resemble that of the 1970s. In fact, it may be much more challenging, since the oil crisis that now looms before us will likely be far more severe than those of the 1970s. The energy crises of the 1970s were temporary. Unless our society quickly develops alternative energy sources, this crisis will be permanent.

As the crisis progresses, there will be opportunities for individuals to make absolute fortunes from the right investments. In a later chapter, we will cover in more detail how to develop an investment portfolio that should outperform over the next few years. But the important point to remember is that your investment success will depend on how well you can adapt to the changing environment.

Over the next few years, some investors will suffer poor returns because they are still caught up in the habits and beliefs they acquired in the 1990s. Similarly, virtually every financial adviser and pension fund manager will estimate future returns based on the average long-term performance of various asset classes, and the average long-term inflation rate. These are:

Asset class	Large-cap stocks	Mid-term government bonds	U.S. T-bills (cash equivalent)
Geometric mean return 1/1/26–7/31/05	10.4%	5.3%	3.7%
Average inflation rate	3%	3%	3%
Real return	7.4%	2.3%	0.7%

Assuming an investor divides his savings equally among stocks, bonds, and cash, he or she would expect to make a real return of 40 percent over the next ten years. However, if inflation were to average 7 percent, as it did in the 1970s, the investor would instead lose 0.5 percent a year. (Actually, he would lose more than 0.5 percent, because these returns do not take various fees into account.) And if inflation in the coming decade turns out to be higher than it was in the 1970s, millions of retired persons will find themselves in desperate situations as their savings evaporate.

In fact, if inflation reaches double digits, over the next decade and perhaps beyond, most people will have a difficult time creating a prosperous life for their families. Life will be similar to the 1970s, but with the volume turned up. Energy will become ever more scarce and expensive. Unemployment will reach record heights. The price of all consumer goods will skyrocket. Stocks will be volatile and most securities will produce negative real returns.

Of course, if you are one of those few investors who know how to spot the biggest financial opportunities, and have acquired the skills to invest successfully in volatile markets, you should be able to create far greater wealth than you have today. The key, as we have said before, is to free yourself of groupthink and develop an open mind.

We must issue one warning, however. It is important, in your enthusiasm for the potential profits you can make, not to forget the long-term seriousness of the situation. The energy crisis will lead to huge changes in our society, voluntary or otherwise. We believe civilization can save itself from utter collapse, but there is no guarantee. Moreover, there may be much hardship along the way. So before we look at the best-case scenario, we will consider what the world will eventually look like as a consequence of a permanently declining oil supply.

CHAPTER 10

The World of Tomorrow: Decline, Stasis, or Armageddon?

On August 29, 2005, America had a rare opportunity to witness what can happen when a complex society is suddenly stripped of its ability to maintain complexity. Hurricane Katrina slammed into New Orleans with a ferocity equal to multiple nuclear explosions. All the systems put in place to maintain the survival, comfort, and security of people living in a modern civilization—power, sewage, water, food distribution, law and order, medicine, government, commerce—were gone in a matter of hours. When rescue helicopters arrived on the scene two days later, they found "total chaos. No food, no water, no bathrooms, no nothing. . . . no structure, no organization, no command center."[16]

The death and destruction were horrifying, but in some ways understandable. The awesome power of Nature is something with which human beings periodically come face-to-face. What was

---

16. Quoted in "Images of Devastation, Anguish and Survival; New Orleans, August 30, 2005," *Newsweek*, September 12, 2005.

shocking, to those who were not actually present, was how quickly the city's residents abandoned a lifetime of social conditioning and reverted to barbarism.

As *Newsweek* put it, "The news could not have been more dispiriting: The reports of gunfire at medical-relief helicopters. The stories of pirates capturing rescue boats. The reports of police standing and watching looters—or joining them. The TV images of hundreds and thousands of people, mostly black and poor, trapped in the shadow of the Superdome. And most horrific: the photographs of dead people floating facedown in the sewage or sitting in wheelchairs where they died, some from lack of water. . . . By Thursday, New Orleans was on the verge of anarchy."

In the days that followed, many would point fingers of blame at various levels of government for having failed to maintain levees, to plan adequately, or to respond quickly enough to prevent the disintegration of society. We, too, were tempted to blame the chaos that followed the storm on a failure of leadership. Perhaps our leaders neglected to prepare for such an emergency, and responded so slowly, because they were either foolishly confident such a disaster would never happen, or because they were preoccupied with a different set of problems and goals. Perhaps they were so much in "crisis mode" already that other concerns fell by the wayside. As we mentioned earlier, groupthink often arises because a small group of decision-makers is under so much pressure to solve a particular problem that they lose sight of the big picture. Hence, they forget to expect and prepare for the unexpected.

A second explanation that occurred to us, which is even more disturbing, was that perhaps our society has reached the stage where the business of solving problems has begun to suffer from diminishing returns. In other words, maybe it no longer seems practical to guard against disasters that might not happen or are a long way off. Of course, that is a formula for disaster, because eventually one or more potential disasters will surely rise up and catch society unprepared.

False Hope from Technology

Our concern, as you know by now, is not so much with natural disasters, which generally affect one particular place for a brief time (albeit with long-lasting effects). What keeps us awake at night is the threat of the growing energy crisis that, if our civilization does not deal with it in time, will affect every community on earth and last forever.

What will happen when oil supplies fall behind demand? We have built our modern civilization on the premise of unending growth—growth that needs energy. We have built a complex civilization that requires increasingly larger amounts of energy to maintain itself. What happens if growth is no longer possible? What if, just like the Easter Islanders, we start to run out of the resources needed to build bigger statues (or cities)? What if even maintaining the cities we have today becomes too expensive?

Curiously, when faced with a terrifying prospect—for instance, a sudden frightening event in a horror movie—a common human response is to shut one's eyes. The loss of civilization, and the resulting vulnerability most of us would experience, is an equally frightening prospect that provokes an instinctive desire to become shortsighted, if not completely blind.

The situation is rather like being a member of the Donner Party, that infamous expedition whose members became trapped by heavy snow in the Sierra Nevada in 1846 and were forced to resort to cannibalism. Imagine the oil supply today is the Donner Party's last crate of food. The leaders know the food will eventually run out, and when it does, they may be forced to do the unthinkable, or else have it done to them. But that reality is so frightening that, instead of working out a logical plan for survival, their response is to pretend the problem does not exist, or else reassure everyone with irrational statements like, "Don't worry, we can live all winter on body fat alone," "Someone with a wagonload of groceries will find us in time," "There's a lot more food in that crate than you might think," or "We're working on a new type of blender that will extract more nutrients from the remaining food."

For example, a common argument today is that new technologies will save us from the threat of an oil crisis by increasing oil production. According to Daniel Yergin, author of *The Prize*, "The ultimate amount [of energy] available to us is determined both by economics and technology. . . . If you pay smart people enough money, they'll figure out all sorts of ways to get the oil you need."[17] Such an argument might be valid if we were talking about how to build a better mousetrap. But it makes no sense when talking about oil. The earth's crust contains only so much oil that can be extracted for a reasonable cost, and no amount of money or brains can change that fact.

Yergin and others point to new technologies such as 3-D seismic imaging, new deepwater drilling techniques and equipment, and the development of exotic energy supplies such as liquefied natural gas and oil sands as ways of increasing energy production. Notes Yergin, "People think of the oil industry as this backward, nineteenth-century industry with people randomly drilling holes. But in fact, next to the military, it's emerged as probably the biggest consumer of computer technology in the world."[18]

Sadly, Yergin and his allies are living in a fantasy. The increasing use of high technology in the oil industry only proves our point. Technology is expensive. If the world were truly awash in oil, as the optimists claim, there would be no need to spend vast millions of dollars on seismic imaging and high-tech drill rigs in order to exploit the most hard-to-reach deposits. Truthfully, the reason the oil industry needs all that technology is because oil is becoming more difficult to find and extract. We are already pumping all we can from the deposits that were easy to find and

17. Quoted in "Why We'll Never Run Out of Oil," by Curtis Rist, *Discover*, June 1999.
18. Ibid.

cheap to pump. Now we are forced to turn to deposits that are more costly to find, and more costly to pump. Eventually the costs will exceed the rewards.

Just consider that since 1970, oil prices have gone from under $3 a barrel to over $60. That has given the United States a tremendous incentive to increase production. The United States is the richest and most technologically advanced country in the world. Americans (at least the leaders) know that their prosperous lifestyle depends on maintaining an unlimited supply of inexpensive oil. And yet all our technology has been unable to prevent the decline in U.S. oil production over the past thirty-five years. Money and brains cannot repeal basic geological laws.

The situation is similar to the problem of nuclear waste. No matter how much money we put into solving the problem of nuclear waste, the laws of physics are inviolable. Nuclear waste gives off radiation as the nuclei of atoms break apart. The nucleus of an atom is held together by the strong nuclear force, so the radiation released when it breaks is more than a match for the electromagnetic force, which is a hundred times weaker. Since any container we can build is held together by the electromagnetic force, it is only a matter of time before the nuclear waste inside destroys the container and escapes.

Geological laws are just as strongly enforced by Nature. Once we extract half the endowment of an oil deposit, technology may help us control the rate at which production declines, but it cannot stop the decline. That is the brilliance of Hubbert's law, which technology has failed to disprove. Since there is only a finite number of economic oil patches in the world, global oil production must eventually decline. In fact, even if production simply flattens, that will be enough to prevent future economic growth.

Clearly, the oil crisis will force our civilization to change. Our concern is how it will change, and what our leaders can do to reduce suffering during the change.

Facing Facts: Our Possible
Decline and Fall

We noted in chapter 3 that there are several possible outcomes when a civilization faces a crisis that results from resource limits and declining returns from complexity. The first option is a loss of complexity. This is not the preferred option, since it means a good deal of hardship. Nor does it do the leaders of the society much credit, since it is the option that will be forced upon them if they fail to plan for a better outcome. Nonetheless, as the example of the former Soviet Union shows, if the leadership remains intact long enough to supervise the transition to a lower level of complexity, civilization can survive.

James Howard Kunstler, in his book *The Long Emergency* (the title of which refers to the decline in oil supplies), paints a vivid picture of how the approaching energy crisis could force American society to become less complex:

> The scale of all human enterprises will contract with the energy supply. We will be compelled by the circumstances of the Long Emergency to conduct the activities of daily life on a smaller scale, whether we like it or not, and the only intelligent course of action is to prepare for it. The downscaling of America is the single most important task facing the American people. As energy supplies decline, the complexity of human enterprise will also decline in all fields, and the most technologically complex systems will be the ones most subject to dysfunction and collapse—including national and state governments. Complex systems based on far-flung resource supply chains and long-range transport will be especially vulnerable. Producing food will become a problem of supreme urgency.
>
> The U.S. economy of the decades to come will center on farming, not high-tech, or "information," or "services," or space travel, or tourism, or finance. All other activities

will be secondary to food production, which will require much more human labor.

Kunstler believes the suburban lifestyle (which he calls "the greatest misallocation of resources in the history of the world") will be impossible to sustain in a world of increasingly expensive oil. As energy becomes more costly, few people will be able to afford to heat a 5,000-square-foot home, or to own a car—let alone drive ten miles to and from work each day. It will be cost-prohibitive to ship goods from China, or even food from out of state, to supply suburban neighborhoods, so the malls and box stores will be empty.

In place of suburbs, Kunstler envisions American society devolving back into a form similar to that of the nineteenth century, when most people lived on farms or in small towns—a lifestyle not unlike that of the Amish today. Modern agriculture, which depends on oil for fertilizer, pesticides, herbicides, and machinery, would be replaced by old-fashioned, labor-intensive farming.

In a world of declining energy, the only government would be local. Highways and commercial buildings would fall into disrepair. The only industry possible would be cottage industry. People would be forced to repair things rather than buy new ones. Finding enough land for local food production would be difficult. Most middle-class, professional jobs would be gone. Schools would be smaller, and education past the eighth grade would be rare.

The vision of the future Kunstler offers is bleak, but also somewhat romanticized. He does not hide his dislike of suburbs, large corporations, globalization, government, and the other social institutions he imagines will pass away. We suspect he might welcome a return to small towns with locally owned businesses and old-fashioned civic values.

If Kunstler is right about anything, it is that our civilization is built on oil. The oil crisis may arrive far more gradually than Hurricane Katrina, but if it catches us unprepared, the loss of complexity could be devastating. Without cheap energy, our civilization would be unable to sustain itself much above the nineteenth-century level. In fact, it will be difficult to do even that, since we no longer have an infrastructure that works without cheap oil. Few people today have the knowledge or the skills to grow food, make clothes, manufacture items, repair tools, or build houses the way their great-great-grandparents did. Self-sufficient family farms have become exceedingly rare.

However, we disagree with Kunstler's pessimistic appraisal that nothing can be done to prevent a serious decline in complexity. Kunstler unfairly dismisses the notion that our society could ease the transition away from oil, as well as preserve a high level of complexity, by developing alternative energies. In actuality, alternative energies exist right now, backed by proven technology, which we could use to sustain civilization well into the future. The only question is whether we will put them in place in time.

Civilization is not inevitably doomed. The problem is that too many individuals are either living in denial concerning the approaching crisis, or else too willing to give up without a fight. What we can do, and need to do, is develop a workable plan to cope with the decline in oil production. We can save our civilization if we are willing to put serious effort into producing enough energy from alternative sources to replace the decline in oil, and if we start now.

On the other hand, if we continue to ignore the problem, the loss of complexity could be far more devastating than a return to pre-automobile small-town life. A real decline in complexity would mean shortages of food and other items, a breakdown of law and order, and a corresponding reign of terror. Malnutrition and starvation, especially in the North, could be widespread, resulting in a much lower population. Diseases would be harder to prevent and control. Cities and towns across the continent might come to look like New Orleans after Katrina. Civilization could truly collapse.

Securing Our Long-Term Survival

A second possible outcome, one that assumes our leaders are a little more farsighted than Kunstler imagines, would be for civilization to move toward a level of complexity that matches our long-term, sustainable energy production. We noted earlier that some societies, such as Tikopia and Japan, were able to avoid collapse by limiting their consumption of resources to within the boundaries of sustainable production. Some ecological economists argue that the solution to the energy problem is for the entire world to follow a similar practice. The result would be zero economic growth, but it would also prevent collapse.

According to Herman Daly, a University of Maryland economist, a zero-growth society does not mean an end to wealth creation. We could in fact move to an economy in which qualitative improvements supersede quantitative gains, where increases in wealth or quality of life per capita could be achieved with improved product design rather than higher consumption. It would, however, mean a cap on resource consumption, and a limit on population growth. It might also mean, as Kunstler suggests, returning to an economy where products are designed to last longer, and be easily repaired, in order to make better use of resources.[19]

Daly argues that the transition to zero growth is imperative given our current ecological and resource constraints. While there is no doubt that this new world would indeed be novel, it would not necessarily be all bad. We would have to give up the attitude that success in life is defined by how many possessions one has by the time one dies. But there are other ways by which we could measure success. Unemployment might rise, but the world as a whole would be breathing cleaner air and perhaps spending more time at home.

Daly, furthermore, cites some of the abundant research on

---

19. Herman E. Daly, "Economics in a Full World," *Scientific American*, September 2005.

human contentment that points out that after obtaining relatively modest amounts of money, more money does not buy more happiness. Of course, this does not rule out that some people are still likely to be wealthier than others. (We will point out in later chapters how to remain at the top of the heap, at least for the coming decade.)

Daly, like many academics, is concerned mostly with preventing environmental destruction rather than avoiding a chronic shortage of energy. However, there is a point where preservation of both our civilization and the environment dovetail. Clearly, it is better to maintain as much complexity as we can than to suffer the fate of the Roman Empire and fall into barbarism and a second Dark Age. The long-term maintenance of civilization depends on a healthy environment as well as a secure energy supply. Zero growth may offer us the best option for survival.

However, we fully appreciate that the transition to a zero-growth society would likely bring about a host of problems. In the first place, it would mean considerable changes to our culture. We would have to learn to see higher consumption as immoral and measure progress more in terms of quality and efficiency. We would have to learn to cooperate more with other nations. In a zero-growth world, no nation could consume more than its fair share of the world's resources without facing reprisals.

It takes courage to rewrite traditional values when they no longer serve the interest of our survival. Some civilizations, such as the Greenland Norse and the Easter Islanders, fell because they could not do it. The Japanese and the Tikopians survived because they were more practical, more flexible. Perhaps Americans would be up to the task, but it would be a challenge.

It is also difficult to imagine that we could become a zero-growth world without incurring one or more severe recessions along the way. Any government or organization of governments attempting to manage such a dramatic transformation smoothly would need to have a much higher level of competence than any in human history.

In addition, a zero-growth society would hardly fulfill most people's dreams and desires. What most people want, us included, is to enjoy the promise, if not the reality, of a middle-class or higher lifestyle. We want enough energy available to support that goal.

Fortunately, there is a third choice that might satisfy. The best-case scenario is neither zero growth nor a decline in complexity, but instead to develop new energy sources that can augment and even replace oil. Just as the development of coal saved England from falling wood production, and brought about the Industrial Revolution, new energy sources are the only option that could let us enjoy more economic growth and a higher level of complexity. In fact, even a less complex or zero-growth society will eventually need new energy sources to replace the dwindling supply of oil. So in any case, humanity will be better off by developing alternative energy as soon as possible.

In the next chapter, we will look at the best alternative energy options—those that are already proven. However, let us first point out two more reasons why their development will be essential.

The Biggest Threats

In 1985, the world had a spare oil capacity of 8.7 million barrels a day. That is how much extra oil could have been produced if it was needed. It also meant that if one country suffered an unexpected drop in production, due to an accident or political unrest, other countries could make up the difference. But in recent years, almost all the spare capacity has disappeared, leaving oil supplies much more vulnerable.

Consider, for example, that two hurricanes in 2005, Katrina and Rita, reduced oil production by 1.5 million bpd, creating a bona fide energy emergency. In the past, we would have expected the price of oil to decline following such storms. Exogenous shocks have rarely had much lasting effect, and natural disasters like hurricanes had little impact on global energy markets. But in the weeks following Katrina and Rita, despite seasonal weakness in oil demand and slightly lower demand from China, oil prices remained stubbornly high.

If a mere 1.5 million bpd can have such a big impact on the cost of oil, that means any single oil-producing country has an equal ability to affect global energy prices. From now on, any oil-producing country that suffers turmoil, or decides to suspend exports for political reasons, could create a bigger jump in oil prices than OPEC did in the 1970s.

Imagine how much higher oil prices would rise, for instance, if terrorists were to deliver a major blow to the oil production capacity of Kuwait, or Iraq, or Saudi Arabia. What if Venezuela or Iran were to suspend oil exports in retaliation for U.S. foreign policies? What if civil war erupts in Nigeria? It would be so much easier now than in the 1970s to create a major energy crisis.

In addition, peaceful relations among nations may be more difficult to maintain as the oil shortage grows. Just as starving people will fight over any remaining foodstuffs, occasionally even reaching the extreme point of consuming each other, as the energy crisis unfolds, desperate nations may become more vicious in their competition for the remaining oil supplies. As Kunstler points out:

> How do we suppose that China and the U.S. will continue to enjoy cozy trade relations at the same time they become desperate rivals contesting for control of the regions that possess the world's dwindling oil supplies? One hardly need point out that the military struggle has already commenced, with the U.S. desperately running its Middle East police station in Iraq, not to mention the Central Asian an-

nexes in Afghanistan and several former Soviet Republics. Both Uzbekistan and Kyrgyzstan have agitated for America to remove its bases, while China and Russia egg them on in the background.

So far, China has stopped short of military adventuring, but they have sent agents scurrying around the world to secure oil-supply contracts with many of America's leading suppliers, including Canada and Venezuela, and they are pursuing civil-engineering works all over Africa to forge happy future energy supply relations.

In the past few years, a dispute has arisen over some 5.3 billion cubic feet of natural gas reserves located under the East China Sea, in an area claimed by both China and Japan. In the summer of 2005, the Chinese company CNOOC received a contract from the Chinese government to conduct exploration in the disputed area, much to the annoyance of Japan. Meanwhile, Russia and China held military exercises nearby, which many interpreted as a signal that China was willing to defend its claim. Most likely, the United States will support Japan if the dispute escalates, but the last thing we need now is a war with China.

Another area of contention is Iran, and its program to develop nuclear reactors—possibly to aid in creating nuclear weapons, but also for energy production. The United States and Europe have been attempting to persuade Iran by various means to end its program, while Russia and China appear to support Iran's right to the technology. India and Pakistan have nuclear weapons now, and North Korea may continue pursuing them as well. In other words, the world is becoming more dangerous.

Energy is essential to wealth. Just as the United States will feel compelled to defend its access to oil, other nations, who feel they have an equal right to enjoy a share of the world's wealth, may fight to secure some of the remaining oil deposits. With nuclear weapons becoming more widespread, the possibility of nuclear war grows greater, and with it the most dramatic, large-scale collapse of civilization the world has ever witnessed. As Albert Einstein observed, "I don't know what kind of weapons will be used in the third world war, assuming there will be a third world war. But I can tell you what the fourth world war will be fought with—stone clubs."

In other words, it may not be enough for the United States to secure an abundant supply of energy for itself. To preserve civilization from destructive conflicts, including possibly nuclear war, the entire world needs to move toward greater energy equality and security—and perhaps a more even distribution of energy and wealth.

By far the best way to avoid the threat of nuclear war and the resulting mutual self-destruction is for new energy supplies to be developed that give most citizens of the world the hope of a reasonably abundant lifestyle. Before we are forced to spend copious amounts of wealth fighting each other, we should spend it on making conflict unnecessary.

Eventually, oil prices above $200 will force the world, through the action of the free market, to consume less oil and to rely more on alternative energies. The faster we can develop sustainable energy, the less hardship there will be in coming years. And even if we must transit to a less complex society, alternative energy will make the change easier and require less of a drop.

However, there is one problem. Putting alternative and sustainable energy supplies in place will take time—decades, in fact. The effort required will also be huge—on the scale of fighting a major war. Unless we get started almost immediately—and even immediately may be too late—our chances of success are slim.

CHAPTER 11

Planning for Survival: Alternatives to Oil

The downfall of civilization, whether it occurs overnight because of nuclear war, or slowly because of ever-increasing energy prices, is something we must avoid at all costs. Civilization may be imperfect, but it provides tremendous benefits for our children, for our elderly, for the sick and disabled—in short, for all of us at some point in our lives. As Thomas Hobbes argues in *Leviathan* (1651), without civilization, when "men live without other security, than what their own strength and their own invention shall furnish them," the result is "no arts; no letters; no society; and which is worst of all, continual fear, and danger of violent death; and the life of man, solitary, poor, nasty, brutish, and short."

The biggest threat our civilization faces is that since the early 1970s, we have been losing control over our essential oil supply. Having burned through more than half of America's oil reserves, we have become increasingly dependent on foreign oil imports to keep up with demand. Morcover, even if we attempted to assert control over the rest of the planet, it is doubtful we could force production levels high enough to meet the growing needs of the world economy. The petroleum inheritance of humanity is literally fixed in stone. Experience tells us that once half is spent, Nature will force us to budget the rest.

To those who have studied history, our need to develop new and alternative energy sources to supplement oil production has been obvious for a long time. In 1988, Joseph Tainter, while discussing the fall of past civilizations, noted:

> Even if the point of diminishing returns to our present form of industrialism has not yet been reached, that point will inevitably arrive. Recent history seems to indicate that we have at least reached declining returns for our reliance on fossil fuels, and possibly for some raw materials. A new energy subsidy is necessary if a declining standard of living and future global collapse are to be averted.
>
> . . . Here indeed is a paradox: a disastrous condition that all decry may force us to tolerate a situation of declining marginal returns long enough to achieve a temporary solution to it. This reprieve must be used rationally to seek for and develop the new energy source(s) that will be necessary to maintain economic well-being. This research and development must be an item of the highest priority, even if, as predicted, this requires reallocation of resources from other economic sectors. . . . I will not enter the political foray by suggesting whether this be funded privately or publicly, only that funded it must be.

We can speculate that the "disastrous condition" Tainter refers to may be the failure of energy supplies to meet demand. Now that this disaster is on our doorstep, his proposed solution still makes sense. Our society may not be able to increase oil production much further, but it does have control over how it sets priorities and how it spends its resources over the next decade. Putting those resources into developing new energy supplies would relieve far more suffering in the future than, for example, making further spaceflights to the Moon.

As an analogy, suppose your town occupies a patch of land where the only source of freshwater is the town well. As your community expands, it draws more and more water from the well each day. Eventually, the water level in the well starts to decline, and some people become concerned that the well could one day run dry.

Meanwhile, the town has good evidence that a new well could be dug on an unowned patch of land nearby, and a pipeline built to bring additional water to the town. The downside is that it will take considerable time, effort, and expense to build the new well and pipeline. But afterward, the town would have plentiful and inexpensive water for the foreseeable future.

The town council thus faces the following dilemma: On the one hand, the town well might never run dry, in which case building the new well would be an unnecessary expense that takes money away from other projects. On the other hand, if the town well does run dry, and there is no new well in place, everyone would die of thirst before they could dig a new well.

No one really knows what the future will bring, but if we were in charge of such a town, we think it would be better to build the second well before the first one runs dry. The added safety margin would be worth the extra expense.

The same is true about oil today. No one is one hundred percent certain how much oil is left in the ground, how expensive it will be to extract, or how high demand for oil will grow long-term. While the world will never completely run out of oil, oil will become increasingly difficult and expensive to extract, to the point where diminishing returns make further production increases unaffordable, and worldwide production begins to decline. Maybe we will reach that point in another decade or two. Maybe we will reach it in a year or two. Maybe we are already there.

What we do know is that demand for oil is increasing at the same time that many oil fields have passed their peak, and few new ones of any size are being discovered. We know that, outside of OPEC nations, production is already declining. So it only makes sense to put effort and resources into developing alternative energy sources now, while conventional sources are still relatively inexpensive. Left too late, the cost of developing alternatives may become prohibitive.

The Barrier of Preconceptions

Perhaps the greatest tragedy, if indeed we come to tragedy, is that the collapse of civilization could have been avoided. Perhaps we cannot continue consuming energy at the same rate, nor will any nation in the future match our current level of consumption. Yet there is no need for civilization to suffer a total collapse. Replacing a significant amount of oil with other forms of energy is a realistic goal that will help us preserve a higher level of complexity for generations to come.

As we have tried to convey in earlier chapters, society's biggest barrier to coping with the energy crisis is not a lack of alternatives, but our own preconceptions that blind us to both the problem and possible solutions. There is, for instance, a widespread belief (no doubt the result of groupthink) that renewable energies are not worth the effort to develop, that they are novelties that will never be able to compete economically with oil, or power anything bigger than a pocket calculator. A softer version of this admits that alternative energies might someday answer our energy needs, but says it will take decades of research and development before they become reliable or efficient enough to be worth putting into widespread use.

These beliefs are based on the notion that oil prices will average near $30 a barrel for many decades to come. We grant that if oil prices remain stable and low, there is less incentive to develop alternatives. However, as we have already explained, oil prices are unlikely to ever again be as low as they were a few years ago.

Some alternative energies are disapproved of by environmentalist sympathizers on the grounds that they create too much pollution or are inherently dangerous. On the other hand, some clean, renewable forms of energy carry a negative stigma because people associate them with hippies, environmental activists, and other radical, non-mainstream thinkers. Oil, by comparison, is as much a part of mainstream, conservative America as ten-gallon hats, fast cars, baseball, and Thanksgiving turkey. It is what "real" men living in the "real" world make "real" money from.

Not only are all these preconceptions incorrect, they unfortunately act as a barrier to solving the energy crisis. In truth, abundant, reliable energy sources exist that not only are becoming less expensive than oil, but could also bring a host of other benefits, including solid profits for the developers. Some of them are non-polluting, and some of them are less polluting than they used to be, thanks to new technology.

However, we cannot afford to reject any alternatives, even the dirtier ones. The world today consumes energy at a steady 13 terawatts (13 trillion watts), 85 percent of which comes from fossil fuels. By 2050, experts expect demand to increase by another 30 TW.[20] As oil prices rise, society will need all the alternative energy it can find in order to prevent collapse. If we must use some dirtier sources temporarily until we can build the infrastructure for renewable energies, it will be worth it to prevent the immense hardship that could otherwise result.

The Most Promising Solution

One of the most promising alternative energies, which has yet to receive the respect it deserves, is wind. In August 2001, two

---

20. Robert F. Service, "Is It Time to Shoot for the Sun?" *Science*, July 22, 2005.

Stanford engineering professors, Mark Jacobson and Gilbert Masters, wrote a one-page article in the journal *Science* titled "Exploiting Wind Versus Coal." *Science* is no soapbox for environmentalists. It is one of the most respected academic journals in the world. Every article published in *Science* goes through a very stringent peer review, so you can be sure the mathematics are sound.

In the article, the authors point out that the type of windmills we are building today can compete economically with coal as a way to produce electricity. Specifically, while one can produce electricity from both coal and wind at a cost of roughly 4 cents a kilowatt-hour, the extra health care and environmental costs resulting from burning coal raise the total price of electricity from that source to between 5.5 and 8.3 cents. Wind, which is a very clean technology, creates no health care costs, and is thus the less expensive choice.

The article generated a great deal of controversy, but eventually even its most strident critics admitted that wind was at least competitive with other forms of energy. Furthermore, as oil prices surpass $100 a barrel, and with natural gas (which trades at roughly a 7:1 ratio with oil) over $10 per MMBtu, wind will become the cheapest way to generate electricity from now on.

Two years after Jacobson's article was published, the British House of Lords released a study on alternative energies. The study also concludes that wind is nearly as cheap as natural gas. However, there is a critical difference between Britain and the United States. In the United States, natural gas costs roughly 50 percent more than in Britain. In other words, windmills may now be able to produce electricity for half the cost of natural gas generators. In addition, some sources project that the cost of wind generation will fall as much as 50 percent over the next few years.[21] In light of the overwhelming evidence that oil and natural gas prices are

---

21. Jeremy Rifkin, *The Hydrogen Economy* (New York: Jeremy P. Tarcher/Penguin), 187.

headed dramatically higher, windmills are a compelling alternative to coal, oil, and natural gas–fired generators.

Another aspect to wind is even more exciting. In recent years, researchers have been speculating that someday we may be able to use hydrogen in place of petroleum as a fuel for automobiles, airplanes, and similar applications where stored energy is required. In the case of cars, several manufacturers are currently developing vehicles equipped with hydrogen fuel cells that convert hydrogen to electricity, which would then power an electric motor. Until recently, the one drawback has been that hydrogen does not naturally occur in accessible deposits, the way oil does. Instead, hydrogen must be produced from coal, natural gas, or simple water—using electrolysis.

Electrolysis is a proven, hundred-year-old process that generates both hydrogen and oxygen. It is so simple that high school teachers often demonstrate the process in science classes. Electrolysis involves immersing two electrodes in pure water, to which an electrolyte has been added, and running direct electrical current through them. Oxygen then bubbles up from the negative electrode, while hydrogen bubbles up from the positive electrode. The only drawback is that electrolysis requires electricity, which brings us back to the problem of how to produce electricity.

Until recently, we believed that the hydrogen economy was decades away because of the cost of producing hydrogen without fossil fuels. However, in 2005, Mark Jacobson and two associates published another study in *Science* showing that it has now become economical to generate hydrogen, through electrolysis, using electricity generated by windmills. Adding up all costs over a ten-year period, Jacobson estimates that wind energy could be converted into hydrogen fuel at a cost of between $3 and $7.40 per kilogram of hydrogen.[22]

---

22. M. Z. Jacobson, W. G. Colella, and D. M. Golden, "Cleaning the Air and Improving Health with Hydrogen Fuel-Cell Vehicles," *Science*, June 24, 2005.

When hydrogen is then used as fuel in a vehicle powered by a hydrogen fuel cell, the price would be equivalent to paying between $1.12 and $3.20 per gallon of gasoline or diesel. Since drivers in certain parts of the United States paid over $3 a gallon for gasoline in 2005, this means wind is now a competitive alternate fuel for automobiles. Clearly, as the price of oil continues to rise, *hydrogen from wind will be considerably less expensive than gasoline.*

Planning for Survival

In addition to lowering the price of energy, generating our transportation fuel from the wind/electricity/hydrogen cycle would also allow us to reap immediate health care savings due to a huge reduction in air pollution. By using hydrogen fuel, our society would save at least $100 billion in health care costs, and save as many as 6,400 lives each year.

Of course, there is a catch. The conversion to hydrogen fuel would require the government to put in place a clear, well-defined plan, and marshal a good portion of our society's resources to executing it. We would have to build not just windmills, but also the infrastructure to support a fleet of hydrogen-powered cars. This may not be as daunting as it seems. It may be possible to equip service stations with small facilities that can produce hydrogen from electricity and water, utilities to which they are already hooked up. Wind farms would then feed electricity into the grid. Nonetheless, it would be a huge project.

Jacobson told us in an interview that he estimates that *the cost of building enough wind turbines to completely fill America's fuel needs would be in excess of a trillion dollars.* That is roughly equal, in today's dollars, to the money we spent in the endeavor to win the Second World War. Saving ourselves from an energy shortfall will be a similar major endeavor, but one that is absolutely necessary.

The Necessary Alternatives

Wind is an appealing alternative energy because it is clean and plentiful, and because the technology is already proven. However, wind alone will not answer all our needs. To ensure adequate energy supplies in future years, we will need to exploit other potential sources as well, if only to buy ourselves time while we create an infrastructure to support renewable energy.

Probably the second most promising energy source is coal. Coal is certainly the dirtiest of all fossil fuels. The *Economist*, in fact, branded it "Environmental Enemy No. 1" in its July 6, 2002, issue, and most environmentally conscious people recoil at the idea of its continued use. However, 25 percent of the world's coal reserves are within the United States, so we do have a good supply of it. Techniques for converting coal into a motor fuel ("coal gasification") have been around since 1980. In addition, new technologies have been developed that can considerably reduce the pollution that results from coal. "Clean" coal, however, costs more to produce than regular coal. In fact, the reason coal gasification is not more widespread already is that it could not compete in the late 1980s and 1990s, when oil was under $25. However, as oil prices continue to rise, making fuel from coal will become increasingly economical.

Of course, coal—like oil—is a fossil fuel whose production is subject to similar diminishing returns. One study that applied Hubbert's Peak to North American coal production found that coal production will likely peak in the year 2035. The study assumes that North American natural gas production peaked in 2002, and worldwide oil production will peak in 2010.[23] So we may only have another thirty years before coal production also enters a permanent decline.

It is a well-documented fact that coal is more costly than its

---

23. Gregson Vaux, "The Peak in U.S. Coal Production," *From the Wilderness*, May 27, 2004, http://www.fromthewilderness.com/free/ww3/052504_coal_peak.html

actual price. As we noted earlier, the health care costs resulting from coal are at least $100 billion a year. Jacobson, responding to a letter regarding his article, notes that coal and natural gas have received heavy subsidies in the past, and still do today, subsidies that include "exploration and mining tax credits, preferential loan interest rates for fossil-fuel power plants, long-term utility contract subsidies to coal, gas pipeline subsidies, and greater federal funding of coal- and natural gas-technology programs, not to mention portions of the cost of monitoring of pollution attributable to these industries."[24]

Moreover, there is the problem that coal requires a lot of water to both mine and ship. We could easily be substituting one scarce resource, oil, for another, water. And then there are all the costs associated with pollution.

By necessity coal will continue to contribute to energy production. However, we cannot count on its ability to take over from oil. What coal we use from now on should probably be clean coal, to save on environmental costs, and we must be mindful that coal production may not increase after the next generation.

A third source we should not overlook is nuclear fission. Part of the reason energy prices fell in the early 1980s was that a number of nuclear power plants came online, generating the equivalent of 3 million bpd of oil. However, accidents such as Three Mile Island and Chernobyl resulted in widespread objection to new nuclear facilities, as well as increased regulatory demands, and so no new reactors have been built since.

We fully admit that nuclear fission has its drawbacks, the top three being the difficulty of disposing of nuclear waste, the risk of accidents, and the use of waste to develop weapons of mass destruction. However, the growing energy crisis could have such a

---

24. Mark Z. Jacobson and Gilbert M. Masters, "Response," Letters, *Science*, November 2, 2001.

devastating effect on civilization that the benefits of additional nuclear power plants would outweigh the risks. Fission could be used temporarily—say, for a generation or so—while other energy sources are being perfected.

Eventually, however, we will be forced to give up nuclear fission permanently. Fission reactors require uranium, which is a resource in far shorter supply than oil. At the moment, proven reserves and recoverable resources of uranium only amount to between 3.4 and 17 million metric tons respectively. To produce an additional 10TW of electricity from nuclear plants would require 10,000 new nuclear reactors. We would have to build a new 1GW (1 gigawatt) reactor every two days for the next fifty years. And even then, 10,000 reactors would use up all the known uranium supplies within six to thirty years.[25]

Scientists generally regard nuclear fusion as potentially a better source of energy than fission, since it will produce less nuclear waste. However, no one has yet figured out how to make fusion work. The most promising project at the moment is an experimental fusion reactor currently being built in France. It is expected to cost $5 billion to construct, and no one can say whether it will work once it is finished. Even if it does work, it will create a fusion reaction that will last for only 500 seconds at most.[26] Most likely, fusion will not become a source of energy for at least another fifty years.

Also in the category of sources that will not be useful for some time is solar energy. Solar energy is very appealing because it is clean and quiet, and because there is a lot of energy in sunlight. Unfortunately, today's solar cells are inefficient, converting no more than 10 percent of the light that hits them into electricity. To make solar cells competitive with electricity generated from

25. Martin I. Hoffert et al, "Advanced Technology Paths to Global Climate Stability: Energy for a Greenhouse Planet," *Science*, November 1, 2002.
26. Robert F. Service, "Is It Time to Shoot for the Sun?" *Science*, July 22, 2005.

fossil fuels, either the efficiency of solar cells needs to be greatly increased, or the cost of making them would have to fall 50 percent. In addition, generating 20TW of electricity with today's solar technology would require covering 0.16 percent of the earth's land surface with solar panels—a considerable undertaking. Until the technology improves, solar energy will remain a niche method of making electricity.

Certain "exotic" fossil fuels may make a greater contribution to solving our energy needs in the future. Natural gas, like oil and coal, is also a diminishing resource. We are unlikely to be able to increase gas production fast enough to meet future demand. However, gas is now becoming an important source of electrical power in the United States, with 80 percent of new power plants being gas-fired. Currently, we are building the infrastructure necessary to import liquefied natural gas (LNG) from other countries. We estimate that over the next fifteen years, LNG could add the equivalent of 5 to 6 million barrels of oil a day to the world's energy supply. This is not a huge contribution, but it will help.

Additional fuel will come from the tar sands located mainly in Canada and Venezuela. Extracting oil from tar sands is more difficult and expensive than pumping it from wells. Historically, there have been cost overruns in developing tar sands, and there are also environmental issues. Obtaining oil from the sands also requires energy, so as oil prices rise, so do mining costs. However, tar sands contain 66 percent of the world's oil reserves, so, provided extraction costs stay below the price of oil, they will contribute to world oil supplies.

Another exotic fuel category is liquid fuels made from plants, such as ethanol and biodiesel. The Energy Policy Act of 2005 requires use of these fuels in America to reach 7.5 billion gallons by 2012. Most ethanol is made from corn, which is an expensive crop to grow. Biodiesel is made from vegetable oil, and currently costs around $5 a gallon. The industry hopes to perfect a method of making biofuels from waste material such as cornstalks and wood chips, which may bring the price down. However, more research needs to be done first.[27]

Government and the War Against the Energy Shortfall

None of the energies available, including oil, will single-handedly be able to satisfy the world's growing energy needs. We will need all of them to ensure that civilization survives. Moreover, this is not a crisis that can be solved by any one corporation or consortium. No corporation will be able to devote the $1 trillion needed to develop sufficient supplies of alternative energy to safeguard the nation from declining oil production, and no bank will be willing to finance such a project as long as the world stays in denial about the problem.

Only a massive effort by the federal government will be able to solve the energy crisis. The resources government must marshal will be no less than what were required to fight World War II. In fact, that is how government must treat this task. The War Against the Energy Shortfall will be the most important government campaign of the twenty-first century, because if it fails, civilization will fail.

As with World War II, the government needs to quickly prepare a comprehensive plan that encourages the fastest development of all possible energy sources. Just as the interstate highway system could not have been built without government, government must now plan and finance the creation of an alternative energy infrastructure. It must offer enormous tax incentives to companies that can develop alternative energy sources. It may need to commandeer resources, taking them away from less important areas. And it may need to take steps to discourage the overconsumption of oil.

---

27. Naila Moreira, "Growing Expectations: New Technology Could Turn Fuel into a Bumper Crop," *Science News*, October 1, 2005.

Such a plan will take a lot more than money and legislation. It would require our society to rewrite many of its beliefs and attitudes. Our leaders must begin by acknowledging the problem. They must be willing to stand up and announce publicly that an energy crisis is approaching—that oil production is topping and that the American way of life cannot continue without new sources of energy. Government agencies will need to stop glossing over the real problems and challenges. The media will need to give airtime to the problem. Both academic and corporate America must be enlisted to develop a workable plan for the transition.

By taking these steps, our leaders would harness people's instinct to trust authority, and direct it in a positive way toward solving the problem. Respect for authority and conforming to one's peers are only bad if the group and its leaders are in denial about a real problem and realistic solutions. If our leaders are open-minded, and look at the situation honestly, with an ample amount of perspective, then we stand a chance of maintaining complexity in the face of declining oil supplies. In addition, we will likely recover the cost of developing alternative energies over the long haul through energy savings—especially given the likelihood of $200 oil.

The American people have a history of making great strides when focused solidly on a specific goal. What more important goal could there be than preserving our way of life, which depends on energy?

It is especially urgent that we begin this task immediately. Bringing new energy supplies to market cannot be achieved overnight. It can take a decade, for instance, to build a new nuclear facility. Some energy sources need more research before we can even begin to develop them. Wind turbines can be constructed in less than twenty-four months, and without highly skilled labor. However, the sheer number of windmills we need to build will make their construction a lengthy process.

For example, right now the United States produces half its electricity supply from coal, and 96 percent of the coal we consume is used to make electricity. Jacobson estimates that to replace 10 percent of our coal consumption (roughly 5 percent of our electricity supply) with wind would require between 36,000 and 40,000 windmills. To meet all our electricity needs from wind would therefore require twenty times that number, and likely take more than a decade to construct. It will also require setting land aside for wind farms, and providing money for their construction.

The amount of time, money, and effort required to free ourselves from dependency on oil is huge. Yet if we do not commit to it immediately, we could easily go the way of past civilizations that closed their minds to reality and postponed dealing with problems until it was too late.

How tragic it would be if our civilization were to share the fate of the Roman Empire, when all along the alternative energies were available that would have enabled us to survive. Just as we are tempted to shake our heads at the stupidity of the Easter Islanders cutting down their last tree, how ironic it would be if future historians, studying the downfall of Western civilization, were to shake their heads in disbelief that we could have neglected to develop new energy sources when oil production was clearly about to decline.

The errors of groupthink, and the experiments by Milgram and Asch, continue to haunt our civilization. They represent crucibles that we just may not be able to pass. But what makes the human species unique is our ability, on occasion at least, to surmount our inherent weaknesses and change our behavior. If we want our civilization to have a future, we must find the courage to make such a choice today.

Postscript

For the most part, our aim with this book is to equip individual readers and investors with the information they need to survive and thrive in the coming energy crisis. We have tried to avoid entering the realm of political activism. However, it would be nice to think that, as a result of this book, some people may become inspired to raise awareness of the crisis among their peers and political leaders.

As the crisis unfolds over the next few years, many citizens will feel angry over high energy prices, not to mention inflation. They may demand that the government take steps to artificially lower oil prices. This, however, would only postpone the inevitable catastrophe and make recovering from it more difficult. On the other hand, lobbying our leaders to fund the development of alternative energy sources that can adequately meet our country's future needs would be far more beneficial. The sooner we can put a significant amount of alternative energy into production, the more secure our future will be.

If you believe as we do that the approaching energy crisis is one of the most important problems facing the United States and the world economy, and wish to do your part, then we recommend you tell everyone you know—including your congressional representatives—to read Mark Jacobson's articles on wind very carefully and to support the development of alternative energies. They offer the best chance we know for survival.

As we will illustrate in the next chapter, our country's leaders seem to lack awareness of the danger facing us. They need citizens to alert them.

CHAPTER 12

Misplaced Priorities:
Our Biggest Obstacle Today

Before proceeding further, we must emphasize that if we did not think society had a chance of saving itself we would not be writing this book. Nonetheless, we are concerned that most authorities today are ignoring the growing problem of tightening oil supplies, and are thereby endangering our future.

Of course, this is not the first time a group consensus on oil has proven false. In the late 1970s and early 1980s, when oil prices were peaking, most experts were convinced they would remain high, and climb higher. In fact, it is interesting to note that many of the experts who were the most bullish on oil prices thirty-five years ago, just before prices started to fall, now have every confidence that oil will remain plentiful and cheap for the foreseeable future.

For example, Daniel Yergin coauthored an article in a 1979 issue of *Foreign Affairs* stating that the energy problem would become "an energy emergency that will persist throughout the entire 1980s."[28] You may recall that we mentioned Yergin in an

---

28. Robert Stobaugh and Daniel Yergin, "Energy: An Emergency Telescoped," *Foreign Affairs* 58, no. 3 (1979).

earlier chapter as one of those who now claim the amount of oil available is limitless, needing only more money and technology to bring it to market.

In 1981, the International Energy Agency stated, "In moving towards 1990, the industrialized countries will be walking an oil tightrope." Since then, the IEA has changed its mind, and now agrees with Yergin. According to the IEA's executive director, Claude Mandil, "There is no shortage of oil and gas in the ground, but quenching the world's thirst for them will call for major investment in modern technologies."[29]

Similarly, the U.S. Department of Energy, in its National Energy Plan II (1979), said, "Any surplus production capacity that individual OPEC countries may have developed in recent years will almost certainly vanish by the mid-1980s, perhaps sooner. . . . In 1990 prices, adjusted for future inflation, oil could be selling for $42 to $55 a barrel." In this case, their projections were correct, but premature. OPEC spare capacity did disappear, and oil prices did pass $55, but not until 2005, fifteen years later than the department expected.

However, rather than taking credit for being partially right, the Energy Department has now decided they were wrong all along and oil prices will stay below $35. As of October, 2005, the department's Web site displayed the following prediction: "The average annual world oil price, measured as the U.S. average refiners' acquisition cost of imported crude oil (RAC), in real (inflation-adjusted) year 2003 dollars will rise from $27.73 per barrel in 2003 to $35 per barrel in 2004, and then decline to $25 per barrel by 2010 as new domestic and imported supplies enter the market."

Just as these authorities and experts (and many others like them) were completely wrong about the direction of oil in 1980,

---

29. International Energy Agency (IEA), "Resources to Reserves—Oil and Gas Technologies for the Energy Markets of the Future," press release, September 22, 2005.

we believe they are equally wrong today. Back then, they underestimated potential oil production. Today, they seem to be overestimating it. Why should this be? Once again, we suspect the answer lies in groupthink and conformity.

Just as participants in the Asch experiments felt pressure to agree with group opinion, even when it was clearly wrong, experts in 1980 likely felt pressure to project higher oil prices. After all, oil had been rising for a decade. Everyone expected oil would keep rising; that was the groupthink of the time. It did not matter that the energy crises of the 1970s had resulted from politics rather than supply constraints, nor that nuclear plants were either built or scheduled to be put into production that would add the equivalent of about 3 million bpd, or about 5 percent of the world's energy supply. If any expert had predicted oil prices would fall, he would have been dismissed as unrealistic. People would have asked him what planet he had been living on. On the other hand, if he predicted higher oil prices, everyone would judge his ideas as sound. Even after such predictions proved wrong, very little blame was leveled at any expert, because the entire group made the same mistake.

It is an unfortunate effect of groupthink that most authorities are afraid to voice an unpopular belief because they are afraid of being wrong and losing face. Similarly, when Wall Street analysts make predictions, those predictions are part of public record. If an analyst's prediction disagrees with the majority, and the majority turns out to be right, the analyst's credibility is shattered. The same is true for academics, many of whom have been shunned and ridiculed by their peers for voicing a radical idea. Being proved right years later, perhaps after you are dead, is little consolation. Sadly, it is safer to be wrong in a crowd than to be the lone voice who is right.

We ourselves know that writing a book like this invites a degree of derision from mainstream commentators, especially if it turns out we are less than one hundred percent correct. Nonetheless, the evidence we are right is so strong, and the suffering that could result from the energy crisis is so great, that we have decided the risk is acceptable.

During the 1990s, the world became accustomed to stable oil prices. Consequently, mainstream opinion today is that they will remain between $25 and $45 a barrel, for many years to come. For any analyst or government agency to disagree with that, regardless of the facts, would be as difficult as a Swarthmore student defying group opinion and identifying the longest line. It is a remarkable affirmation of Asch's brilliant work that not one sell-side analyst on Wall Street, not one major government official, and not one CEO of a major oil company today dares to disagree with the long-term view that oil will settle back into a $25 to $45 range.

Unfortunately, when Wall Street analysts talk, investors are not the only ones who listen. The heads of companies pay heed as well. Were the head of a major oil company, for example, to propose financing an alternative energy project based on the assumption that oil prices were going to be significantly higher three years forward, today's Wall Street analysts would turn their thumbs down. They would lower their earnings estimates for the company. The stock would suffer, and so would the company's access to funds.

Yet until we accept the fact that oil and natural gas are in long-term uptrends, we have no hope of convincing industry and the government—and it will take a consortium of both—to start spending more than a trillion dollars on the necessary infrastructure to develop alternatives to fossil fuels.

We have said it several times now: in order to prevent the hardship of the coming oil crisis, the movers and shakers in America need to become more open-minded. They need to stop projecting from the recent past and look at the present situation with open eyes, armed with a broad perspective on energy and the history of civilization. They also need to take action, now. Unfortunately, we see very few signs that our leaders are willing to do what is needed.

Government's Misguided Approach

To solve our long-term energy needs, our society needs to move away from oil, which has begun to show signs of diminishing returns on investment, and focus on developing alternative energy. Yet for the most part, our government continues to direct its efforts toward supporting increased oil production. It has accepted the idea that oil and gasoline should be priced at much lower levels than currently prevail. Indeed, current policies are geared toward perpetuating the myth that cheap oil and gasoline will exist in perpetuity.

However, although most people today feel that $3 a gallon for gasoline is outrageously high, the truth is that gasoline is currently underpriced compared to its fundamentals. *If free-market forces were allowed to determine the price, Americans today would be paying between $5.60 and $15.14 a gallon for gas.*

The reason gasoline prices are actually very low is that gasoline is heavily subsidized. According to the International Center for Technology Assessment, federal and state governments provide a total of between $9.1 billion and $17.8 billion in tax breaks to the oil industry to help domestic companies stay competitive and keep American gas prices low. Federal tax breaks include:

Percentage depletion allowance	$784 million to $1 billion
Nonconventional Fuel Production Credit	$769 million to $900 million
Immediate expensing of exploration and development costs	$200 million to $255 million
Enhanced Oil Recovery Credit	$26.3 million to $100 million
Foreign tax credits	$1.11 billion to $3.4 billion
Foreign income deferrals	$183 million to $318 million
Accelerated depreciation allowances	$1 billion to $4.5 billion

Many states impose a lower sales tax on gasoline than on other products, giving a further subsidy of $4.8 billion. The Taxpayer Relief Act of 1997 gives another $2.07 billion in breaks. In addition, since state income taxes are based on federal taxes, that reduces the oil industry's taxes by another $125 million to $323 million a year.

It is not that we are in favor of high taxes, but when government unfairly taxes one industry less than others, the result is not only a violation of the spirit of free enterprise, it also causes a misallocation of society's resources. However, there is more.

Apart from tax breaks, the government subsidizes the oil industry in other ways. These include $36 billion to $114.6 billion that the government spends each year to build and maintain roads and bridges (without which people might drive less), up to $220 million a year on research and development subsidies, $311.9 million on export financing subsidies, $227 million on oil resources management programs, and $270 million on support from the Army Corps of Engineers. Some argue that the government also picks up the tab for as much as $942.9 billion every year for the environmental, health, and social costs related to oil use. And these are only a few of the many subsidies oil producers enjoy. We have not even mentioned the additional subsidies for coal and natural gas production.

Consider, for example, the federal energy bill that was passed in July of 2005. The bill provides some $14.5 billion in tax breaks, most of which benefit oil producers, even though they are enjoying strong profits, thanks to rising prices for their product. Only $2.7 billion worth of tax breaks went to alternative energy production. As we pointed out earlier, weaning the nation off its dependency on imported oil could require an investment of $1 trillion. So this bill really provides next to nothing toward that goal.

Many of the pro-environmental, anti-oil commentators complained that the bill provides no incentive to reduce oil consumption, such as making cars more fuel-efficient. Nor does it require utilities to generate a percentage of electricity from alternative sources. We, on the other hand, would argue that if the government simply ended the subsidies to oil, the resulting high fuel prices would provide the incentive needed to get car manufacturers to improve efficiency, utilities to start building wind farms and other alternative energy sources, and ordinary citizens to start conserving energy. If we are truly close to Hubbert's Peak, providing incentives to consume more oil, which is what the current subsidies do, is an act of self-destruction. It is akin to a person, stranded in the Arctic in wintertime with only two weeks' worth of firewood, deciding to burn it all the first night.

Last year, I spoke at a conference at the Boulders in Arizona. It is a beautiful place, and all the leading public finance bankers in the country attended the conference. These are the people in charge of raising money for public works—everything ranging from coal-fired utilities to nuclear plants to wind farms. I was privileged to be one of the keynote speakers. I spoke about the perils of our energy situation and our urgent need to begin developing alternatives. I detailed the advantages of wind. I was almost pleading with my audience to do something—for the sake of their children. No one disagreed with my conclusions, and the organizer of the convention told me it was one of the best speeches, if not the best, ever given.

You may wonder, since the speech was so well received and convincing, whether the attendees then decided to raise the hundreds of billions of dollars needed to fund the alternative energy projects. Unfortunately, the answer is no.

In some respects, my thirty-minute speech was like a microcosm of the Milgram and Asch experiments. I became a temporary authority figure to the crowd. Everyone accepted the authority figure and agreed with one another. Yet once the speech was over, I became simply one voice among a herd of analysts, all of whom repeated what most bankers were saying—that the current rise in oil prices was destined to be ephemeral.

Keep in mind, throwing massive amounts of money into an alternative energy project makes no sense if you believe that oil is going to be trading at $30 five years from now. In order to commit the hundreds of billions of dollars needed to finance an alternative energy infrastructure, companies and bankers must first believe that oil prices will remain in an uptrend for the foreseeable future. Otherwise, their massive investment could turn into a massive loss.

One of the other speakers at the conference was Bill Kristol, a former adviser to Dan Quayle who is widely regarded as one of the brightest people in Washington. Indeed, Kristol graduated magna cum laude from Harvard and went on to receive a PhD from Harvard in political science. He is the editor of the widely read Washington insider magazine the *Weekly Standard*. In his speech, Kristol emphasized that America needs a real issue to focus on, and that one of our problems since the cold war is that we have not had such an issue.

After the speech, I spoke to Bill Kristol, and asked him specifically, "What about energy as an issue?" He vehemently disagreed, noting that oil was a very small part of GDP, that we had been down that road before, and that the current situation was no different from the end of the 1970s. I tried my best to convince him otherwise. I pointed out that although oil today might be a small part of GDP, it is an essential part, and that as prices rise it will become ever more important. Eventually, as in the 1970s, it will set off an inflationary spiral. However, unlike the 1970s, there will be no alternative energy coming onstream and no real hope for new oil either. I tried as hard as I could to convince him, but to no avail. I have no doubt Kristol is a brilliant man, but like most people in government, he has fallen victim to the group-think that no permanent shortage of oil could ever occur.

It is the same attitude as expressed by the secretary of energy, Spencer Abraham, in remarks he made at the National Energy Summit in 2001: "America's current energy supply crisis is not due to some inevitable neo-Malthusian depletion of resources. The United States—and our North American and hemispheric neighbors—are blessed with a rich abundance of natural re-sources. It's political leadership that has been scarce."[30]

In his remarks, Abraham blamed the energy problem on the Clinton administration, claiming it excessively taxed demand and limited supply. (He failed to mention that the Clinton adminis-tration, like the current one, heavily subsidized oil.) His proposed solution was to make it easier for Americans to consume more oil and gas by removing regulations and building more pipelines and refineries. Yet that is just throwing more logs on the fire, and ex-hausting the woodpile faster.

Better to remove subsidies and let oil prices be set by the mar-ket. Better to let people experience the real costs of burning oil at the current rate. Only then will our society make a real effort to develop alternatives.

Self-Interested Consumers: Pro and Con

As the oil crisis unfolds, one attitude we can count on to continue will be the self-interest of the average American. The government can channel this attitude in either a helpful or an unhelpful way.

For example, if the government tries to discourage consump-tion by artificially raising energy prices, the results could be un-fortunate. Taxing one particular energy use, such as gasoline, might lead to less consumption of gasoline. However, the decline in gasoline consumption would keep oil prices lower than market forces would otherwise dictate, resulting in greater consumption of oil for other purposes and less incentive to develop alternatives. We need to give decision-makers as much incentive as possible to develop alternative energy. And the best way to do that is simply

---

30. Spencer Abraham, "A National Report on America's Energy Crisis," remarks by U.S. Secretary of Energy Spencer Abraham, U.S. Chamber of Commerce, National En-ergy Summit, March 19, 2001.

to allow declining global production to force oil prices higher. Some taxation of energy might be acceptable if the government uses the revenue to fund an alternative energy infrastructure. However, it would be counterproductive if it were done solely to discourage consumption.

On the other hand, letting gasoline prices quickly rise to double-digit levels, as determined by the market, would encourage people to conserve energy, and to buy products that are more energy-efficient. The energy crises of the 1970s inspired much interest and research, often by nonprofit organizations and academics, in energy efficiency and conservation. After several decades, the results are some very impressive and proven conservation methods, which most of the world has managed to ignore.

For example, Armory B. Lovins, cofounder of the Rocky Mountain Institute, points out that many energy-efficient appliances now cost the same as inefficient models. Houses and buildings have been designed and built that need no furnace or air-conditioning to maintain room temperature, and consume no more electricity than a 100-watt light bulb. Concept cars have been designed with carbon-composite bodies that use 66 percent less gasoline, without compromising comfort, safety, and performance, and without costing more.[31]

Owning a house and car based on the latest energy-saving principles would put a substantial amount of money into anyone's pocket. So why are the streets of every town in America filled with gas-guzzling SUVs parked outside homes with massive furnaces and air-conditioning units? Because energy prices stayed relatively low and stable for so long, the average consumer does not worry enough about costs to make energy efficiency a high priority when choosing a home or car. However, if the government allows gasoline and electricity prices to skyrocket in

---

31. Armory B. Lovins, "More Profit with Less Carbon," *Scientific American*, September 2005.

coming years, self-interest will drive people toward buying the most fuel-efficient car they can find. They will want the house that is least expensive to heat, and stays comfortable without air-conditioning.

Decreasing consumption in this manner will be helpful. It will stretch out the remaining oil reserves a little, giving us more time to develop alternatives. Yet it will not take the focus off the real problem. Soaring energy prices would provide incentive to develop alternative sources.

The self-interest of consumers can also be detrimental, however. Many people are already upset about rising gasoline prices. As the trend toward higher prices continues, they will probably grow more vocal in demanding that the government do something to bring gas prices back down. The government will feel great pressure to respond by increasing subsidies to oil companies, which will in turn enable people to continue using too much oil, and will discourage the development of alternatives. This is a trap our government must resist, because it is based on the false notion that oil supplies can be increased at will. Keeping gasoline prices artificially low will only bring about a serious energy shortfall much sooner.

The Self-Serving Industry

Oil companies are a popular target for environmentalists and socialists to throw stones at. One would expect, however, that oil companies would have a better than average understanding of energy fundamentals. Turns out they do, as I discovered recently when I spoke to a group of executives, some of whom run the biggest independent energy companies in North America.

I began by outlining the case for a protracted rise in oil prices. I included much of the information presented earlier in this book. I argued that most of the country did not truly appreciate the seriousness of the situation, and that oil prices of $200 or more were likely. Soon, all the oil executives listening were nodding in agreement and showing signs they anticipated that great times lay ahead for them.

The next part of my speech dealt with our need to develop alternative energies, including wind. At that point, I might as well have been speaking to the wind, instead of endorsing it. The audience was polite, but to say they were unenthusiastic would be to understate their reaction. Underlying their response was an attitude that if oil and gas prices rise to exorbitant levels, that would be just fine, since they would make fortunes. There was no concern whatsoever for the damaging effects runaway oil would have on the economy and on the lives of most Americans.

I was a little disappointed, but not surprised. Their reaction is a form of closed-mindedness in which a group—admittedly a very intelligent group—cannot see beyond their own narrow interests and grasp the broader picture. It is an example of groupthink in which members of the oil industry have reinforced each other's views and formed a consensus that the higher oil is, the better it is. Focusing on their own profits, they have failed to recognize the potential disaster—namely, what type of world will emerge if energy becomes virtually unaffordable for most of the applications that benefit average people and keep our economy running.

While we do not want to venture too much into politics, groupthink within the oil industry and its friends may explain why someone like Matt Simmons, the country's leading energy banker and an adviser to both Dick Cheney and George W. Bush, has had so little impact. (As we mentioned in an earlier chapter, Simmons's book *Twilight in the Desert* argues that Saudi Arabia may be on the cusp of a catastrophic drop in oil production.) Clearly, the rational response would be to pay him some heed and pass an energy bill that provides more than just a piddling amount to alternative energies. We fear, however, that it may take a severe crisis before government will develop the courage to act against the narrow interests of the oil industry and promote alternative energies, and by then it may be too late to prevent hardship.

Academic Hyperopia

If corporate America and its allies are unwilling to consider alternatives to oil, surely one might expect the academic community to be more open-minded, to put the health of society as a whole ahead of personal profits, and to consider alternative solutions.

Unfortunately, while the academic community and its allies often are willing to challenge the corporate agenda and consider the interests of the majority, we find that many of them appear equally blind to the immediate problem of energy supply. Specifically, academia's big concern is pollution and the need to prevent environmental degradation. This may be a serious issue, but if an environmental crisis occurs, it will not be for another fifty years. Meanwhile, academia seems oblivious to the present-day threat of an energy crisis that could potentially cause the downfall of civilization long before environmental erosion could possibly do the same.

For example, Bjorn Lomborg, an associate professor of statistics at the University of Aarhus and the director of the Danish Environmental Assessment Institute, recently published a book called *Global Crises, Global Solutions*. Lomborg's book contains a collection of essays written by notable academics, including four Nobel Prize winners, concerning what Lomborg considers the ten greatest challenges the world faces today. These challenges are:

Climate change
Communicable diseases
Conflicts
Access to education
Financial instability
Government corruption
Malnutrition and hunger
Migration
Sanitation
Subsidies and trade barriers

Two things are notable about this list. First, climate change appears at the top. Second, energy does not appear at all.

Similarly, most of the academics we quote in this book are far more concerned with the environment than energy. Jared Diamond, whose analysis of fallen civilizations we cited earlier, provides a list of twelve environmental problems he thinks are most threatening to our civilization. An eventual shortage of fossil fuels is one of the items on his list, but he assumes that oil, coal, and natural gas will remain inexpensive and plentiful for several more decades at least, only then gradually becoming more costly to extract. According to Diamond, deforestation, overfishing, the extinction of species, and soil erosion are far more immediate threats than the energy crisis.

Will Leeb, my son, reviewed Diamond's book for my publication *The Complete Investor*. At seventeen years of age, Will was able to spot Diamond's misplaced priorities. Will notes, "By focusing narrowly on the environment, books such as *Collapse* have the effect of pushing the really big problem, the one with the true potential to make our society collapse—emerging energy shortages—into the background. They help make the debate over alternative energies, such as wind power, seem solely one of environmental correctness. And this no doubt aids and abets many of the world's policymakers to conflate what really is an imminent and civilization-threatening problem—an insufficient supply of oil relative to demand—with problems that can be brushed aside as less immediately threatening, such as global warming."

Herman Daly, whom we cited for his ideas regarding an eventual zero-growth society, is also more concerned with preventing an ecological disaster than an energy shortfall. In addition, I have spoken to a number of Ivy League professors who likewise refuse to acknowledge the seriousness of the energy situation.

The academic consensus (groupthink) is that the environment is the real problem, and that saving the environment depends on getting people to reduce their consumption of oil. Many academics have contributed heroically and brilliantly to the development of alternative energies and energy-efficient technology, but with the aim of reducing pollution caused by oil consumption, not saving civilization from a shortage of energy.

If your aim is to stop pollution, worrying about an oil shortage seems contrary to the cause. Consequently, academia generally accepts the overly optimistic projections of government agencies. We suspect it has forgotten that its very existence depends on a complex civilization, whose survival in turn depends on plentiful energy. We also suspect that many academics find it easier to sound the alarm about a crisis that will not occur until after they retire. Then, if they are wrong, it will not damage their careers.

Of course, the pro-environmental groupthink has its supporters outside academia as well. Bill Clinton, when he was president, gave a number of speeches about the necessity for developing alternative energy. However, he too envisioned the potential crisis as something that exists in an indefinite future. No real effort was made in his presidency to develop alternative energy, and why should there have been, when oil prices were stable? Politicians, generally, concern themselves only with problems that could cost them or their party the next election. At the risk of repeating ourselves, government will likely wait until the crisis is too late to solve before starting to address it.

This is where we stand today: One faction of society's leaders— Wall Street and corporate America—suffers from myopia (short-sightedness), in that they refuse to consider the long-term energy fundamentals or the consequences of a serious energy crisis. The academic and environmentalist community, on the other hand, seems to suffer from hyperopia (farsightedness), an inability to recognize a serious energy crisis when it is close at hand. In the middle are a few lone voices, such as ourselves, wondering how the nation will manage to dedicate the necessary trillion dollars to develop alternative energy if none of our leaders see it as a critical issue.

In all honesty, barring an immediate change of attitude, our chances of avoiding catastrophe are slim.

CHAPTER 13

Your Personal Choice: Insane Wealth or Pitiful Poverty

So far, we have attempted to alert you to the dangers facing Western civilization as a result of the growing energy crisis and the failure of our leaders to acknowledge them or to plan ahead. Make no mistake, the inability of energy supplies to meet soaring demand, and the wave of inflation that will result, is a serious threat. It may, in fact, be the biggest threat we will ever face.

Naturally, this is not a crisis that we, as individual investors, can exert much control over. Government and industry must make a major concerted effort to create an energy supply for the nation that is sustainable in the long run—and that means a campaign to develop alternative energy on a scale equal to fighting a world war. It is far from certain whether they will launch such a campaign in time to save civilization.

Whether or not government can acknowledge the crisis and take the necessary steps to solve it, there will likely be hardship over the next decade. The cost of energy will skyrocket, and so will the price of everything else. Double-digit inflation will eat away at personal savings and make it difficult for the average investor to earn a positive real return. Entitlement programs may be whittled down. Many people will have trouble paying for the necessities of life, such as food, clothing, and shelter. All of this is beyond the control of most investors, many of whom will become poorer as the crisis unfolds.

Nonetheless, not everyone will suffer financial loss. As individuals, we can take steps to safeguard our financial situation during hard times, and even come out considerably far ahead. We expect that certain types of investments will benefit tremendously from inflation and produce phenomenal returns. The small percentage of investors who adjust their portfolios now to favor these investments—while reducing exposure to the most vulnerable sectors—are likely to become insanely wealthy.

That brings us to the second objective we have in writing this book: helping you survive and prosper through the inflationary times ahead, by pointing out which investments will likely be the biggest winners and losers. While we cannot be certain of the future, our knowledge of financial history and current economic trends gives us a pretty sound idea of what to expect.

Making Money When Inflation Soars

As explained in previous chapters, there have been three periods when the inflation rate rose to double digits—1917–20, the 1940s, and 1974–81. Each of these periods was marked by shortages of oil and other resources, and by massive increases in government spending.

We believe that the next ten years will look remarkably like the 1970s. Not only will oil prices reach new heights, well above $100 a barrel, but government spending will increase dramatically too, thanks to demands placed on Social Security by retired baby boomers, as well as America's increasing military needs. As a result, the inflation rate will again exceed 10 percent.

If you were an investor in the 1970s, you will recall that making money was extremely difficult then. Many of the investments generally considered "safe" lost money in real terms (that is, returns minus the inflation rate). Even worse, these so-called safe investments are the ones financial advisers now recommend most strongly to retired persons, or those approaching retirement, who cannot tolerate much risk. They are the investors most vulnerable to market downturns, and as inflation soars once again, they are the very persons who will suffer the most.

On the other hand, people who invested intelligently in the 1970s made healthy returns—and a small handful saw their savings multiply nearly tenfold.

The coming wave of inflation will again divide investors into two groups: those who become steadily poorer, and those who become as rich as Croesus.

Which group you belong to is up to you. You can conform to the prevailing groupthink, but if you do you will suffer financially. In the 1970s, after subtracting inflation, the average investor lost between 1 and 2 percent a year. On the other hand, every $100,000 you put into inflation-advantaged investments could be worth more than $1 million by the time the next ten years are up.

Assuming you want to be one of the few who grow wealthier, let us look now at how the different investment categories fared in the 1970s. This will be your road map for investing in the current decade. We will start with the investments that lost money—the ones you should avoid at all costs.

Investment Pitfall #1: Cash

Table 1 ◆ **How Cash Holdings Fared in the 1970s**

	Average annual nominal return	Average annual real return	Total real return	Change in real $10,000
Cash	6.3%	−1.1%	−10.5%	$8,950

Most people know that keeping your savings in hundred-dollar bills stuck under the mattress or buried in your backyard is not a sound investment strategy. Currency may be handy in an emergency, but it will not grow in value over time the way sound investments will.

Even worse, the effect of inflation is to erode the buying power of money. That is why a dollar does not purchase as much today as it did when you were a child. The higher the inflation rate, the faster the value of your dollars disappears. So in a high-inflation period, cash becomes the worst form of savings.

Of course, when we speak of cash investments, we usually mean savings accounts, CDs, T-bills, and other short-term deposits. These pay a low level of interest that is supposed to make up for losses due to inflation. Unfortunately, in the 1970s, interest rates paid on cash were less than the inflation rate. So while you might have ended the decade with more dollars in your savings account, those dollars would have been worth 10.5 percent less than the amount you started with.

At the moment, the interest rate on three-month T-bills is 3.44 percent. Yet the inflation rate is 3.7 percent. So cash is already a losing proposition.

If you want to be financially secure, stay away from cash.

Investment Pitfall #2: Bonds

Table 2 ◆ How Bonds Fared in the 1970s

	Average annual nominal return	Average annual real return	Total real return	Change in real $10,000
Bonds	5.5%	−1.9%	−17.5%	$8,250

Bonds are the traditional investment vehicle for retired persons and others seeking current income. A bond is a loan made to a government or a corporation that must be paid back when it matures. Bonds pay higher annual interest than cash, and are generally more secure than stocks. Unfortunately, bonds are extremely sensitive to inflation, and that makes them a poor investment today. Let us explain.

When investors lend money, they demand that the income they get from the loan equals the inflation rate plus a reasonable amount of interest. So the higher the inflation rate, the higher the yield on bonds.

The trick to remember about bonds is that price and yield are like two ends of a teeter-totter. As the yield on bonds goes up, the price goes down and vice versa. That means that as inflation rises, bond prices fall.

For example, suppose you own a bond that pays 4.56 percent annual interest. With inflation at 3.7 percent, your bond barely pays you anything in real terms. Let us also suppose the inflation rate rises to 7.7 percent over the next year or two. The yield on your bond is now less than the inflation rate, so you are losing value.

If you decide to sell your bond, the purchaser will want compensation for the increase in inflation. He will want the yield from the bond to be 4 percent higher. And the only way for that to happen is if he pays you a lower price for the bond.

As inflation rose during the 1970s, bond prices fell by an average of 1.9 percent a year. We expect them to be an equally poor investment over the coming decade as well, with one exception.

The Only Bonds Worth Owning from Now On

One type of bond that is worth holding as inflation rises is Treasury Inflation-Protected Securities (TIPS). Unlike with most bonds, the value of TIPS is protected from rising inflation. The principal and interest payments on TIPS automatically increase or decrease according to the inflation rate. The higher the inflation rate, the higher the payments. TIPS also have a built-in protection against deflation. You are guaranteed to get back your principal on maturity.

If you want steady income over the coming years, you can buy TIPS directly from the U.S. Treasury at auction four times a year (January, April, July, and October). Keep in mind that as the consumer price index rises your principal expands, and you will be taxed on the increase.

Another option is to buy units in a TIPS mutual fund, such as the Vanguard Inflation-Protected Securities Fund.

Eventually, we hope the coming wave of inflation will peak, just as it did in the early 1980s. That will be the time to buy long-term bonds heavily, when interest rates on bonds are beginning to fall. But until then avoid all bonds but TIPS.

Investment Pitfall #3: Stocks

Table 3 • How Large-Cap Stocks Fared in the 1970s

	Average annual nominal return	Average annual real return	Total real return	Change in real $10,000
S&P 500	5.9%	−1.5%	−14.0%	$8,600

Our third investment pitfall is the biggest and most dangerous trap. Because of the tremendous gains stocks made during the 1990s, most people have come to regard the stock market as the best, or possibly the only, investment vehicle. Most investors today put too much faith and money into a diversified portfolio of stocks.

This is an example of groupthink that you must resist. Under high inflation, only certain segments of the stock market will do well. The overall market will offer poor returns, and some segments will suffer devastating losses.

In the 1970s, the S&P 500 grew by an average of 5.9 percent a year. But with inflation running at over 7 percent, the real return

Why Inflation Will Cause Stock P/E Ratios to Fall

One effect of rising inflation is that it causes price/earnings ratios to fall across the whole spectrum of stocks. There are two reasons for this phenomenon.

First, inflationary eras are marked by greater uncertainty. When inflation is low, businesses feel confident and optimistic about the future and their growth plans. Investors feel the same about their financial futures as well. But when inflation rises, no one knows how high future prices will be, so investors grow wary of paying too high a price for shares in companies. Hence, P/E ratios fall.

The other reason is that earnings growth has two components: real growth, which comes from actual expansion—new products, new stores, greater market share, greater efficiencies, etc.—and inflationary growth, which means charging higher prices to cover higher costs.

Investors generally do not put as much value on inflationary growth, because it applies equally to all companies. Investors value real growth, because that is what identifies good management.

When a higher proportion of earnings growth is inflationary growth, investors will not pay as much for that growth, so P/E ratios fall.

on the market for the entire decade was a loss of 14 percent. That is worse than even the 1930s, when stocks still gained 20 percent in real terms.

So our first stock recommendation for the near future is to avoid index investing. Forget about diversifying among all sectors. Stay away from index funds, large-cap funds, and any other vehicle that mirrors the broad market. They will only bring you closer to the poorhouse.

Avoiding the Sectors That
Will Be Hardest Hit

Even worse will be the so-called defensive stocks. These are sectors typically viewed as safe havens, because their profits come from things people need in both good times and bad—products such as food, household goods, and personal care items. Because demand for such products is relatively immune to economic fluctuations, the stocks of companies that make them tend to have high P/E ratios.

This will be a deadly combination in the next few years, because during periods of high inflation, price/earnings ratios decline dramatically. In the 1970s, the P/E ratio of the S&P 500 fell from 16 to less than 8. As a result, retail stores, cosmetics, and food stocks all underperformed—with cosmetics leading the plunge with a loss of 45.6 percent. The table below shows what percentage of your money you would have lost in these sectors, and which stocks are most vulnerable today.

Table 4 ♦ Stocks to Avoid as Inflation Rises

	1970 high to 1979 low	
Sectors	*Nominal changes*	*Vulnerable stocks today*
Defensive groups		
Cosmetics	−45.6%	Avon, Elizabeth Arden
Food	−6.0%	Kellogg, Hershey
Retail stores	−34.0%	Federated Stores, Wal-Mart, Kohl's
Double punch groups		
Airlines	−37.0%	AMR, JetBlue
Autos	−55.0%	Ford, General Motors
Chemicals	−47.3%	Dow Chemical, DuPont

The Energy Double Punch

Even worse hit than defensive stocks will be companies whose revenues and profits are inversely related to energy prices. Two prime victims will be airlines and chemical producers. Energy (fuel) is a major cost for airlines, while chemical producers rely on oil as a critical feedstock. These groups suffered massive losses in the 1970s, and are likely to do so again as oil prices soar.

Regarding the automobile industry, the situation is more complex. Car manufacturers were the hardest hit in the 1970s, falling 55 percent. This time around, rising gas prices will likely force a change in American driving habits. Sport utility vehicles will decline in popularity, while fuel-efficient vehicles will become the rage. This will once again hurt U.S. automakers, which have been slow to adapt. Japanese car companies, on the other hand, will likely gain market share.

Investment Pitfall #4: Small-Cap Stocks

Table 5 ◆ How Small Stocks Fared in the 1970s

	Average annual nominal return	Average annual real return	Total real return	Change in real $10,000
Small-cap stocks	11.6%	4.2%	50.9%	$15,090

It may surprise you that we are putting small-cap stocks in the "pitfall" category. Long-term studies have shown that small caps on average produce higher returns than large caps. This was certainly true in the high-inflation period of the 1970s when small-cap stocks trounced the S&P 500 with a total real return of 50.9 percent.

The advantage small caps have traditionally had over large caps is that they can grow their earnings at a faster rate. For example, if a company starts with $100,000 in revenues, it only takes $20,000 in new sales to achieve 20 percent growth. But a company with $1 billion in revenues must find $200 million in new revenues to achieve the same growth rate. In the past, this has made small caps better able to counter both inflation and the lower P/E ratios that result from it.

However, there is a problem this time around. In order for small companies to grow their earnings rapidly, they need access to the world's fastest-growing consumer market. In the 1970s, that was the United States, but today it is not. The fastest-growing consumer market now is the combined market of China and India, or as we call it, "Chindia."

Chindia contains over 35 percent of the world's population. It already has a bigger middle class than does the United States. Yet its per capita consumption of everything is below the world's average and just a small fraction of consumption in high-income countries. Most important, Chindia is growing at four times the rate of developed countries. Even if relative growth rates narrow, Chindia will likely become a high-income region within the next twenty years.

The problem with American small-cap companies is that they are largely excluded from participating in the fast-growing Chindian markets. Instead, they depend on the mature, slower-growing U.S. economy as their source of growth. This puts them at a disadvantage going forward. It means they are unlikely to outperform this time around.

Our recommendation: avoid small-cap stocks as well.

But enough talk of doom and gloom. Now let us turn to ways of making money over the next few years. In fact, let us look at the sectors where investors will make insane profits as inflation rises.

CHAPTER **14**

Making Money in the Coming Collapse

Just as many of the investments traditionally considered safe
will actually be quite detrimental to your savings in coming
years, some of the most downtrodden, unpopular, and underper-
forming investments of the 1990s will produce stellar returns
during the energy crisis. It will be the 1970s all over again, only
more so.

In this chapter, we will look at the investments that will outperform as inflation and energy costs rise. If your opinion of these
downtrodden investments was formed during the 1990s, you
would do well to reassess that opinion. For example, let us begin
with one of the least widely owned investments, often described
as "barbaric" and outdated, that nonetheless is already beginning
to shine once more . . .

Investment Jackpot #1: Gold and Gold Shares

Table 6 ◆ How Gold Stocks and Gold Bullion Fared in the 1970s

Investment	Average annual nominal return	Average annual real return	Total real return	Change in real $10,000
Gold stocks	28.0%	20.6%	550.8%	$65,080
Gold bullion	33.1%	25.7%	884.8%	$98,480

What was the greatest bull market in living memory? Ask most people today, and they would say it was the technology bubble of the 1990s. But they would be wrong.

True, the tech boom was impressive. Between October 1990 and March 2000, the tech-heavy NASDAQ produced annual gains of 34 percent. But this performance holds second place to the bull market in gold that took place in the 1970s.

Gold languishes in times of stable economic growth, when financial assets are in vogue, but when times get tough, gold springs into service as one of the few investments that can get you through.

Gold has always been a hedge against inflation, because the federal government cannot increase the nation's supply of gold at whim, the way it can paper or electronic dollars. So as the value of dollars declines, the price of gold rises.

For this reason, investors should understand that gold is the quintessential inflation hedge. During periods of inflation, it has been one of the only investments to keep pace with rising prices. However, gold is more than just an inflation hedge. When you examine the various economic relationships more closely, it turns out that the real force behind gold's rise is not inflation per se but rather negative real interest rates, which generally accompany inflationary surges. When real rates are negative, you lose money by parking it in cash or in interest-bearing bills or bonds. Thus, money flees to investments that keep pace with inflation, and historically gold has been the surest choice.

You also can get negative real interest rates, however, when deflationary prospects loom. During such times, the Fed will start to cut rates aggressively to ward off deflation, bringing them below price increase levels, and again causing real rates to turn negative. In other words, gold is an essential hedge during periods buffeted by inflationary or deflationary forces alike.

In the early 1970s, gold's price was fixed at $35 an ounce. It began trading freely in 1975 at $200 an ounce and in early 1980 reached its all-time high of $850 on January 21. In real terms, an investment in bullion would have grown to nearly ten times its initial value.

Shares in gold-mining companies had an equally impressive run. From their low in 1970 to their high in 1980, the S&P gold stock index climbed more than eighteen-fold. If you factor in the generous dividends the stocks offered at the time, the decade-long bull market in gold shares produced an average annual return of 37.5 percent—higher than that of the technology bubble.

Of course, the situation was completely the opposite when most of today's investors cut their teeth. In the 1990s, gold suffered a prolonged bear market, reaching a low of close to $250 an ounce in 1999.

Since then, however, gold has entered a new upward trend. As of this writing, it is now trading above $460. But the memory of the 1990s is so strong that few investors currently own gold, or see it as anything more than a raw material for jewelry.

This is another unfortunate example of groupthink that will cause most people to miss what is literally a "golden opportunity." As inflation rises to double digits over the next few years, we expect the present bull market in gold and gold shares will accelerate, eventually becoming as impressive as the one in the 1970s. In fact, gold's rise could be even greater this time, because it started from a position of being despised, undervalued, and underowned.

Gold will regain popularity once people recognize that inflation is on the move. Increasingly, financial advisers will recommend that their clients put 5 percent to 10 percent of their savings into inflation hedges, such as gold and other precious metals. That buying pressure will force the price of gold higher rapidly.

How high could gold go? At its peak in 1980, all the gold in the world both above and below ground (approximately 200,000 tons) was worth about $5.5 trillion, equivalent to around five times the value of the S&P 500 at that time. Today, all the gold in the world represents about 25 percent of the value of the S&P 500.

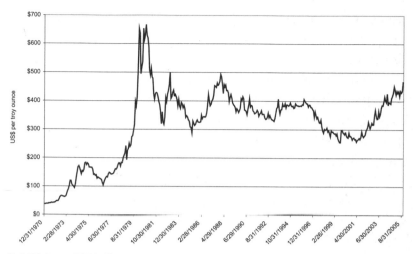

Gold Prices, 1971–Present

Of course, S&P 500 earnings have grown over the past twenty-four years, increasing the index's underlying value. But even adjusting for these profit gains—a little over threefold in real terms—gold today would have to trade at about $2,800 to be on a par with its relative value to stocks in 1980. This would equal a sevenfold gain.

It used to be very inconvenient to invest in gold bullion directly. Bullion had to physically change hands every time a trade was made, and be stored in safe facilities. However, today, a new option has become available for those who want to own bullion: exchange-traded funds (ETFs). For example, one of our favorites is the streetTRACKS Gold Trust (GLD), which invests in actual gold. Similar trusts have traded in London, Sydney, and Johannesburg but they are relatively new to U.S. investors. Each Gold Trust share represents one-tenth of an ounce of gold, less the trust's modest expenses of just 0.4 percent annually. The trust is not actively managed so its expenses should remain very low. To cover those expenses, the trust sells gold on an as-needed basis.

A similar vehicle, the iShares Comex Gold Trust (IAU), has

also been launched recently. While the two ETFs should track each other closely, the volume on the iShares Comex trust is still just a fraction of streetTRACKS Gold Trust's daily average volume of 1.6 million shares over the past six months, making the latter the preferred investment as of this time.

Investing in bullion has some advantages over buying mining shares. Mining companies are riskier investments than the metal, since they can run into unanticipated operational problems. Higher energy prices in the years ahead, for instance, will increase operating costs and put pressure on profits. Tougher environmental regulations also may hinder results. Nonetheless, because stocks are riskier they can provide you with leverage to the price of gold. So it is worth considering gold stocks as an investment too.

At their high in 1980, precious metals stocks represented close to 7 percent of the capitalization of the S&P 500. Yet today the total capitalization of gold, silver, and platinum stocks is roughly $70 billion, or less than 1 percent of the S&P's capitalization. If investors, on average, were to boost their holdings of precious metal shares to just 5 percent of their portfolios, the capitalization of the precious metals sector could easily jump fivefold. So a sevenfold gain that would bring precious metals back to 7 percent of the S&P is not far-fetched.

In a bull market in gold, similar to the one in the 1970s, most gold shares will do well. Just like e-commerce businesses in the late 1990s, there may be many junior gold exploration companies in the coming gold boom whose stock prices grossly overshoot their values. But for cautious investors, the big gold producers will be the safest bet.

Newmont (NEM: NYSE) is the largest American gold miner, and will certainly produce strong returns in the bull market in gold. The company has a strong balance sheet, and it does not hedge (sell forward) any of its gold, which means it will benefit fully as the price of gold rises.

Barrick Gold (ABX: NYSE) is the other major North American gold company. Barrick generates less free cash and is more volatile than Newmont. On the other hand, it should increase its production somewhat faster than Newmont. Barrick had a hedging program, but has been phasing it out.

For diversity across the precious metals spectrum, two of our other favorites are Apex Silver (SIL: AMEX) and Impala Platinum (IMPUY: PK). Alternatively, for a one-stop diversified play you might consider a precious metals fund such as the Tocqueville Gold Fund (TGLDX). But whichever way you choose to participate in the gold bull, your rewards should be more than handsome.

Investment Jackpot #2: Oil and Oil Shares

Table 7 ◆ How Oil and Oil Stocks Fared in the 1970s

Investment	Average annual nominal return	Average annual real return	Total real return	Change in real $10,000
Crude oil	26.4%	19.0%	469.5%	$56,950
Big oil companies	14.2%	6.8%	93.1%	$19,310
Independent oil producers	19.2%	11.8%	205.1%	$30,510
Oil service companies	31.0%	23.6%	732.1%	$83,210

If you have read the earlier chapters on the growing oil crunch, then you know crude oil prices rose considerably in the 1970s, and are likely to do so again in the near future. In fact, the price of oil has already doubled in the last three years. What's more, we expect that this new bull market in energy could last considerably longer, and take prices considerably higher, than the previous one.

Of course, crude oil is even more difficult to invest in directly than gold. Unlike bullion, you cannot purchase crude oil and store it in a safe-deposit box until you are ready to sell it. Trading oil futures contracts profitably requires time and specialized knowledge. So most investors will find it easier to invest in shares of oil companies. Fortunately, as with gold, oil stocks are drastically undervalued at the moment.

Despite the unquestionable fundamentals that underlie today's budding bull market in oil, and despite the fact that oil traded at more than $60 a barrel for much of 2005, every Wall Street firm currently projects that oil will cost no more than $25–$45 a barrel in three to four years' time. (Goldman Sachs recently caused some controversy by saying oil would top $100 a barrel within a few years, but even it expects oil will drop down to the $30 level shortly afterward.) This is groupthink at its most misguided.

As a result of Wall Street's views, oil shares today are priced at a level that assumes $30 oil. That means oil share prices have some catching up to do just to bring them in line with current oil prices, let alone the heights oil will reach as the energy crunch becomes more severe.

As the above table shows, buying shares in the big oil companies back in the 1970s was a very profitable strategy. Those stocks outperformed the S&P significantly, and will do so again in the coming crisis.

Today, the best-known major oil companies are British Petroleum (BP), Chevron (CVX), ExxonMobil (XOM), and Royal Dutch Petroleum (RDPL). They are huge corporations that engage in both upstream operations (exploring for oil and extracting it) and downstream (refining petroleum into gas and producing other products from it).

As oil prices rise, big oil companies earn higher revenues. And when oil prices drop, they still do well, because one of the major costs of their refining operations has fallen. (Lower costs are not always passed on to the consumer.) So if our predictions regarding oil are correct, you will make excellent returns from the majors. And if we are wrong and prices fall, you will have some downside protection. Big oil companies also offer excellent yields, typically twice that of the market.

Of course, independent oil producers made higher gains than the majors in the 1970s, with an average real return for the decade of 205.1 percent. And they probably will again. One of the leading companies in this subsector is Devon Energy (DVN). As one of the most dynamic independent producers of both oil and natural gas, Devon will benefit from price increases in both commodities.

However, there is another way to play the bull market in oil that offers even higher near-term profits.

Why Oil Service Companies Will Soar

From 1970 to 1980, oil service company shares rose more than twenty-fold, almost exactly matching the gains in oil itself. Similarly, during the initial stage of the current bull market—from the end of 1998 to August 2000, when oil prices climbed threefold before reaching an interim peak—the gains in oil service companies nearly equaled those of oil. We conclude that, in bull markets, oil service companies typically rise as much as oil.

However, since September 11, 2001, even though oil and oil service companies both produced strong gains, oil service companies have lagged behind the commodity itself. This is partly because Wall Street—fixated on the idea that oil prices are due to plunge—has not given them the respect they deserve. At some point, when Wall Street finally bows to reality, gains in oil service stocks will start to accelerate dramatically.

How dramatically? To match gains in oil, the service stocks would have to climb more than 60 percent. That is if oil stays where it is. If, as we expect, oil continues to rise, the gains in oil services will be even greater.

If you had to put all your money on just one oil service company, we would recommend Schlumberger (SLB), the hands-down leader in well discovery and management and seismic services. Its clear technological edge is reflected in profit margins far higher than those of its competitors. Historically the stock has traded at a sharp premium to the S&P. In the 1970s, its multiple was twice that of the S&P 500. Today, its premium based on 2006 earnings is only 25 percent, reflecting Wall Street's inability to believe high oil prices are sustainable. If valuations expand to be in line with historical norms, the stock could rise to more than $90.

Moreover, rising valuations for Schlumberger and other oil service stocks would mean those stocks would be bucking a powerful trend. If, as we expect, inflation rises, P/Es for most stocks will drop, making market gains hard to come by. The oil service stocks will be among the rare exceptions, and so could become runaway market leaders.

Of course, the most leveraged oil service companies are the drillers. Three companies, Noble (NE), Nabors (NBR), and Transocean (RIG), cover the gamut of drilling services, and each is tops within its own particular area. Noble is the premier offshore driller, Nabors the premier land driller, and Transocean is the dominant player in deepwater drilling. Each company has far surpassed rivals in every relevant category, from revenue growth to profit growth to profit margins. They should have no trouble maintaining their leadership positions.

In the 1970s, the real return on oil service stocks was 732.1 percent. This time around, the gains could be even greater. For this reason, we recommend that every investor have a stake in oil services.

Investment Jackpot #3: Real Estate

Table 8 ◆ How Real Estate Fared in the 1970s

	Average annual nominal return	Average annual real return	Total real return	Change in real $10,000
Real estate	10.1%	2.7%	30.5%	$13,050
REITs	12.1%	4.7%	58.3%	$15,830

Lately there has been much talk about a housing bubble—and with merit, as mortgages now account for a record and growing portion of homeowners' equity. Homes in many ways are the foundation of consumer finances, much more so than the stock market, which has traditionally been concentrated among a relatively small portion of the population. If the bursting of the tech bubble in 2000 was a rain shower, then a bust of the housing boom today would be a Category 5 hurricane. But that is exactly why we do not think it will happen. On the contrary, we think real estate still has merit as an investment, just as it did in the 1970s.

The trigger that could pop the real estate bubble would be significantly higher interest rates, the kind typically used by the Federal Reserve Bank to slow inflation. But in today's world, with our high levels of debt, an aggressive interest rate policy would run the risk of not just lower real estate prices, but a severe recession. We doubt the Fed is willing to take that gamble. Inflation, though the worst choice for most investors, is the only choice for politicians.

Indeed, high inflation will reduce the economy's dependence on debt. As it further boosts the prices of homes and other real assets, it will diminish the burden of the debt underlying those assets. The same holds true for government as well as individual debt. The government will see the advantage of letting inflation rise and keeping the economy growing. That will maintain tax revenues and make government debt a smaller percentage of the economy—and so more manageable.

Bottom line: real estate was a sound investment in the 1970s, and we think it will remain sound for some time.

Investing in real estate directly often takes specialized knowledge and a great deal of time. Plus, to buy a diversified portfolio of properties takes more money than most investors can afford. Fortunately, there is an easier way to make money in real estate, and that is through real estate investment trusts, or REITs.

The key when choosing a REIT is to focus on those in the most dynamic real estate segments. They will give you the potent combination of capital growth and rising dividends. Lately, some of the best REITs have been those in the business of shopping centers, outlets, and regional malls.

For instance, a REIT we like these days is Regency Centers (REG). It operates a straightforward strategy of owning and operating shopping centers in high-income areas anchored by a dominant grocery store. A conservative balance sheet—a debt to market cap of 31 percent—and one of the best development pipelines in the REIT universe give Regency an edge over its competitors. It funds $300 million a year in new development through strong cash flow generation and its "capital recycling" program, which disposes of the bottom 10 percent of the property portfolio every three years. Given the company's superior real estate portfolio and excellent growth prospects, we think it will continue to perform well.

Investment Jackpot #4: Chindia

We mentioned above that small-cap stocks, which did well in the inflationary wave of the 1970s, will likely underperform due to their lack of access to the huge and fast-growing markets of China and India. Ironically, this situation will give an advantage to certain American large-cap companies—those that are expanding into Chindia.

Inside the vast Chindian market, growth prospects are so immense that even the biggest-cap company can grow its earnings as quickly as a small cap. But only the big caps have strong enough balance sheets and the financial and marketing resources to penetrate that market. So these Chindian stocks will be the equivalent of small caps over the next few years—and an important source of investment returns in the coming inflation wave.

For example, five stocks we think will do extraordinarily well in the next few years are 3M (MMM), Coca-Cola (KO), Intel (INTC), Procter & Gamble (PG), and Texas Instruments (TXN).

Each has already established a powerful beachhead in Chindia. Each is a dominant company in its industry. And each has the financial, marketing, and distribution channels to support continued rapid growth.

Insurance Against Deflation

The above four investment jackpots should produce above-average gains during an inflationary period. But there is another risk you should guard against.

If oil prices rise too rapidly, they could reduce consumer spending and trigger a period of deflation (falling prices) and economic depression. The Federal Reserve must walk a fine line regarding its interest rate policy. It must keep interest rates high enough to attempt to contain inflation, while low enough to maintain economic growth and prevent deflation.

If the Federal Reserve errs, we expect and hope it will err in favor of inflation, since that is the least damaging of the two. We could be wrong, however. Deflation could occur, or there could be several deflationary scares as oil rises faster than the Fed can adjust. Either scenario would mean at least a temporary downturn in precious metals and other inflation-advantaged investments.

For this reason, investors should also own, as insurance, some investments that will make strong gains during deflation. The best choice for this component of your portfolio is zero coupon bonds.

Unlike most bonds, zero coupon bonds (or strip bonds) pay no interest. Instead, you buy them for less than their face value— at a discount—and collect their full face value when they mature.

As we said above, a bond's price and its yield are like two ends of a teeter-totter. During times of deflation, interest rates fall and bond prices rise. The price of zero coupon bonds rises much more than that of most bonds, because a zero coupon bond's yield derives entirely from its discount. That makes them the most profitable investment to own in a deflationary period.

Zero coupon bonds are created through a U.S. Treasury program called STRIPS (Separate Trading of Registered Interest and Principal of Securities). While Treasury securities are never issued as zero coupon bonds, each interest payment for a given bond, as well as the principal, can be separated and traded as a zero coupon security. These are guaranteed by the full faith of the U.S. government. You can buy and hold STRIPS through financial institutions and government securities brokers and dealers.

An even easier way to invest in zero coupon bonds is through a mutual fund that specializes in them. For example, we recommend the American Century zero coupon bond funds, which are easy to buy or sell through discount or online brokers.

◆　　◆　　◆

That completes our reassessment of how various investment groups performed during the 1970s. However, in the energy crisis that is fast approaching, there will be a few differences. Because this energy crisis will be more or less permanent, returns from gold, oil, Chindia, and our other jackpot categories could be much greater than in the 1970s.

In addition, there will be one new jackpot sector this time around that will produce strong returns for investors. Let us look at it now . . .

CHAPTER 15

The Next Hot Investment Sector: Alternative Energy

We noted in an earlier chapter that the biggest barrier to solving the growing supply/demand crisis in oil is the general indifference of Wall Street, government, industry leaders, and most so-called experts. That indifference extends into the area of alternative energy stocks. As long as Wall Street analysts insist oil prices will remain below $45 a barrel long-term, alternative energy companies will be looked on as uneconomical and unworthy investments.

All that will change, however, in coming years when it becomes apparent that oil prices are in a permanent upward trend. As oil supplies fail to meet growing demand, alternative energy will be a huge growth industry, creating tremendous opportunities for investors. In fact, we expect demand for viable alternatives—the most promising of which are wind, nuclear, coal gasification, liquefied natural gas (LNG), and tar sands—will more than match potential supply for years to come. Growth rates for alternative energy companies will be limited only by their ability to supply a voracious market. For some companies, this will mean growth of more than 30 percent a year for the next five years or more. For others, supply constraints will mean somewhat slower growth. Regardless, growth will be accompanied by sharply expanding P/Es as investors embrace the alternative energy sector, and that means excellent profits for those who invest in alternative energy today.

Unfortunately, Wall Street has yet to expressly designate any stocks as alternative energy stocks—an omission that helps explain why energy has become such a problem. If there were dozens of major companies devoted to providing alternative energy, the crisis would be easing. Nonetheless, a few companies have already emerged as leaders in this area, and we think they make excellent investments today.

The Biggest Plays on Wind Energy

The alternative energy with the most potential is wind. It is an inexpensive source of electricity, and the technology is already developed. Today, wind is barely a rounding error in terms of energy production, accounting for less than 1 percent of overall energy usage in the United States. Yet over the past six years, use of wind energy has grown by 30 percent a year. It is only a question of time before wind becomes recognized as critical in meeting our energy needs. We believe the current growth rate is not only sustainable, but could accelerate to 35 percent or more.

The largest wind generation company in America is the FPL Group. Actually, FPL is two distinct companies. The larger, representing some 85 percent of revenues, is a regulated utility operating in Florida, one of the most demographically favorable parts of the country. The company's nonregulated businesses—including nuclear, gas, and wind—account for about 30 percent of its overall profits. Wind represents about a third of this 30 percent, or 10 percent of overall profits.

Because Wall Street has yet to recognize the enormous potential of FPL's deregulated activities, the stock has exceptional risk/reward credentials. The Street estimates five-year growth at

4 to 5 percent, in line with FPL's regulated business. But over the past five years, revenues and income from the unregulated activities have grown by a better than 35 percent clip and now represent about 15 percent of overall revenues, up from 5 percent.

FPL currently has a backlog of wind projects considerably larger than its current wind capacity. The company had chosen to wait for passage of wind tax credit legislation before developing these projects, though they would be profitable regardless. Given the urgent need to conserve fossil fuels, we think the government will eventually provide larger wind tax credits than those now in effect.

Profits from wind should continue to generate outsized growth, pushing overall growth for FPL well into double digits. In addition, FPL Energy has an emerging and potentially very large stake in liquefied natural gas. It has agreements for equity participation in a major LNG terminal and LNG-related pipeline that will serve the Florida area. While these projects are unlikely to begin generating profits before 2008, their implementation would position FPL as a major LNG player and could significantly enhance long-term growth.

The worst case is that FPL will continue to generate moderate growth in dividends and earnings, for total returns of 8 to 9 percent. Much more likely, however, is that growth will increase to the mid-teens, prompting Wall Street to revalue the stock sharply upward. However, a 35 percent growth in wind—and this estimate could prove conservative—could push the utility's overall growth rate well into double digits for this decade, with growth continuing to accelerate after that.

Another fast-growing wind producer is Scottish Power, a Glasgow-based company in the process of transforming itself from a stable but stodgy regulated utility into a major alternative energy provider. Its PPM Energy unit is one of the world's leading wind power generators. Recently Scottish Power sold its U.S. electrical utility, PacifiCorp, to Warren Buffett's MidAmerican Energy

Holdings for $9.4 billion. While the divestiture resulted in a substantial realized loss, it means the company now can focus on its fast-growing U.S.-based PPM Energy division, which accounts for 7 percent of sales, along with its U.K. regulated and competitive energy segment (85 percent of sales).

PPM's earnings have been increasing by 30 to 50 percent a year over the past two years, astonishing numbers in almost any industry and especially for a utility. PPM Energy generates 800 megawatts, primarily in the western United States, with the goal of 2300 megawatts by 2010.

Scottish Power has demonstrated its commitment to PPM Energy by investing nearly £1.4 billion of capital in the division. It also has put significant additional capital into its U.K. renewable energy business, aiming for 1000 megawatts of wind power by 2010.

Scottish Power holds a strong "A" credit rating and through its regulated U.K. business generates enough cash flow to support a 5 percent yield. After adjusting for the PacifiCorp sale, the utility trades at 12.5 times earnings, a discount to its peers. With its high-flying wind power unit driving above-average growth, it deserves a premium multiple. (Note: U.S. investors can invest in Scottish Power by purchasing its American Depository Receipts [ADRs] on the NYSE under the symbol SPI.)

A third leader in the area of wind, along with other alternative energies, is General Electric. Because this ultra-high-quality, triple-A stock is leveraged to prospective chronic shortages of fossil fuels and electricity, GE offers potentially fast-paced growth that will keep you well ahead of inflation.

Jeffrey Immelt, the head of GE, understands the problem of energy supply. While Wall Street is mostly still projecting falling oil prices over the next five years, and most politicians, Republicans and Democrats alike, are paying only lip service to the impending energy crisis, Immelt has helped position GE to play the energy crisis to the hilt.

The company is roughly divided between financial services (about 40 percent of revenues) and nonfinancial services. Within the latter segment, energy-related products—currently accounting for about 12 percent of overall revenues—make up the fastest-growing area. This energy division is widely diversified, and most of its products have leading or dominant market shares in critical areas of energy generation, including almost every important alternative energy technology. While consensus expectations are that the energy division will grow in the low double digits, we think the gains will be considerably higher over the next five years or more, helping to keep overall earnings growth on a fast track.

General Electric is the world's largest integrated wind company and the second-largest maker of wind equipment. Over the past three years, wind revenues, admittedly starting from a small base, have grown by 50 percent a year. The Street projects the percentage growth from this division will be in the low 20s over the next five years. We think it could easily exceed 30 or even 35 percent.

In addition to wind equipment, General Electric is also the leading producer of turbines for coal gasification, which is possibly the next most promising alternative energy. General Electric is also a major player in nuclear energy, producing essential components for nuclear plants, an area that will gain importance in both the United States and abroad. Finally, it is the leading manufacturer of turbines used in standard gas- and coal-powered utilities. In this arena, the company stands to benefit from the near certain shortage in electricity-generating capacity, the aftermath of the bust in capital spending on electricity that followed the boom of the late 1990s.

Altogether, General Electric's energy division could easily grow by more than 20 percent a year over the next decade. As the energy crisis worsens, 25 to 30 percent growth is a possibility. Along with high single-digit or low double-digit growth in its other divisions (such as the company's rapidly expanding stake in infrastructure spending in China), overall growth could easily be in the low teens and even in the mid-teens by the end of the decade, as energy becomes an ever larger share of profits.

In other words, GE offers solid near-term growth that is likely to accelerate, perhaps sharply. With an unmatched combination of quality and growth, it is a one-of-a-kind company that represents one of the best chances we have of successfully negotiating one of the most difficult periods we are ever likely to face.

Capitalizing on Liquefied Natural Gas

The alternative energy source that could make the most immediate contribution to energy supplies is liquified natural gas (LNG). When natural gas is liquefied, importing it becomes a lot more feasible. We estimate that over the next fifteen years it could add the equivalent of 5 to 6 million bpd (barrels of oil per day) to the world's energy supply. Much of this supply, however, will compensate for falling natural gas production.

For instance, over the next five years the United States will need the equivalent of 1.3 million bpd of oil just to replace our declining gas production. The situation is comparable in Western Europe. In other words, LNG will not solve our energy needs but will be a critical supplement. The development process will require perhaps $50 billion to $100 billion in expenditures, on everything from liquefaction processes to terminal construction. Many companies will win big.

General Electric, for example, is in the forefront in turbomachinery, products vital to the liquefied natural gas industry, as well as in the storage and transmission of energy sources such as natural gas. Two other companies we like are Chicago Bridge & Iron (CBI) and Air Products and Chemicals.

Based in the Netherlands, Chicago Bridge & Iron is the engineering and construction firm most leveraged to the world's growing need for new energy supplies. About 80 percent of its business is concentrated within the energy sector. The company's expertise ranges from building LNG terminals to constructing new refineries and retrofitting older ones.

Chicago Bridge & Iron's backlog, revenues, and profits are expanding by about 30 percent a year, mostly from its North American operations. Recently, though, the company has established a position in China, which could further accelerate its already torrid growth. In that event, our long-term estimates of 20 percent annual growth for the company could well prove conservative.

Air Products and Chemicals (APD) is best known as a supplier of industrial, medical, and specialty gases such as oxygen, nitrogen, argon, hydrogen, and helium, and of chemicals such as performance polymers, additives for coatings, lubricants, and corrosion inhibitors. However, it also has a thriving equipment business serving the chemical process, electronics, basic steel, oil, power generation, food, and institutional health care industries. This is the group that will drive the company's growth in the years ahead.

Specifically, Air Products makes heat exchangers used in converting natural gas into a liquefied form that can be stored and shipped. These heat exchangers account for only a small fraction of the company's nearly $8 billion in annual revenue. However, the technology should add several percentage points to the company's growth rate in the next several years.

Air Products is also an important participant in alternative fuels. The company is the principal producer of industrial hydrogen, controlling nearly 50 percent of the market. Hydrogen is essential in refining oil into gasoline and perhaps even more important in developing alternative energies such as shale and tar sands.

During the next five years, we look for APD's profits to grow in the mid-teens, far higher than current Wall Street estimates of about 10 percent.

Other Alternatives

Another source of nonconventional energy will come from Canadian tar sands, which by some estimates contain as much oil as Saudi Arabia. The problem, as we have mentioned before, is that developing the reserves is difficult and costly. Today, the tar sands generate around 1 million bpd of oil. Eventually, yearly production probably can increase by some 200,000 bpd. While this will not make much of a dent in our energy problems, it will provide dynamic growth for companies with major stakes in the tar sands. These companies—which include Petro-Canada (PCZ), Suncor (SU), EnCana (ECA), and Canadian Oil Sands Trust (COSWF)—are perhaps the world's only major oil and gas producers with the ability to raise production over the long haul. Thus, rising prices and production will multiply their profit growth.

Nuclear energy carries a lot of baggage, including public resistance and waste storage concerns. Still, in an energy-starved world, nuclear energy will seem preferable to insufficient energy. Because of the tremendous amount of skill and experience needed to manage nuclear plants, new facilities will go to the most established players—such as Exelon, which is by far the nation's largest nuclear utility. Exelon will benefit as well from rising energy prices, which will improve profit margins on the deregulated portion of its business, consisting largely of the sale of nuclear-generated electricity throughout the United States.

In addition, emerging economies like China and India have little choice but to increase their reliance on nuclear energy, sharply boosting uranium demand. The world's only significant uranium producer is Canada-based Cameco. It stands to benefit from both this tighter market and its own aggressive expansion plans. Trading at nearly twenty times forward earnings, the stock is not cheap for a mine. However, it is very cheap for a company likely to grow by better than 20 percent a year for the next five years.

Two other alternative energies offer some small promise of contributing over the next decade or so. One is coal gasification, which breaks coal down into nonpolluting gases that can be refined into auto fuel. A related and complementary technology is gas to liquid (GTL), which turns natural gas into petroleum substitutes such as diesel fuel. Since diesel is essential to coal mining, GTL will be used to support coal gasification. Together these two technologies could add the equivalent of about 150,000 bpd of oil over the long term.

Air Products and Chemicals is one company that will benefit to some extent from demand for gasification technology. Another is Sasol (SSL). Sasol bills itself as an integrated oil and gas producer with substantial chemical interests. However, a more appropriate view of this South Africa–based company is that it is the world's largest producer of synthetic fuels. Using proprietary technology, Sasol is a leader in coal-to-liquid and gas-to-liquid production. It is also Africa's leading producer of chemicals and chemical feedstocks.

Sasol manufactures syngas from natural gas and low-grade coal. Syngas can be converted into a range of products, including synfuels, which are various blends of low-sulfur diesel fuel. In addition, Sasol produces gasoline, jet fuel, fuel alcohol, illuminating paraffin, and fuel oils, as well as gaseous fuels such as liquefied petroleum gas.

The viability of these synfuels is undeniable: Sasol produces roughly 29 percent of South Africa's fuel needs. However, the company has its sights on far bigger markets with its coal gasification technology. It is targeting both China and the United States, two energy-hungry countries with vast coal reserves.

Wall Street is expecting 15 percent annual growth from Sasol in the years ahead. We think the company's growth will be considerably more.

The Future of Automobiles

As oil approaches $200 a barrel, we shudder to think how high the price of gasoline could go. Those people who are not forced to give up driving altogether will certainly be shopping for more fuel-efficient cars.

Right now, the most fuel-efficient vehicles are hybrid cars. Hybrids combine an electric motor with a gas-burning engine that recharges the batteries during braking. They increase fuel economy by 40 percent or more and are particularly effective in stop-and-go traffic. While hybrids sell at a premium to standard cars, there are many incentives to ownership. Not only do they save on fuel, but owners also enjoy various tax benefits. Other rewards in various localities include unlimited access to lanes generally reserved for high-occupancy vehicles and, in San Jose, California, even exemptions from parking fees. And many hybrid car owners simply want to help the environment and lessen our dependence on Mideast oil.

Investors can profit from hybrid cars first by investing in the car companies themselves. While Ford and GM have made a few inroads in this area, Toyota (TM) and Honda (HMC), the clear leaders, are the best way to go.

Toyota Motor is our favorite conservation play. China, India, and Russia all have sustained double-digit growth in automobiles, and autos are among the products most leveraged to growth in emerging economies. With its exceptional finances—it is one of the few worldwide companies with an AAA credit rating—and extraordinary manufacturing capabilities, Toyota is the carmaker best positioned to provide the huge number of fuel-efficient cars these and other countries will demand. We expect Toyota will become the Wal-Mart of the world's auto industry.

Meanwhile, Honda also is a hybrid player to be reckoned with, with two models in production. The Honda Insight boasts the best highway mileage in the United States at 66 miles per gallon.

The Civic hybrid retains the look of the non-hybrid model but can travel an astounding 650 miles on one tank of gas. In addition, the company is close to releasing one of the hottest-selling cars of the past decade, the Accord, in hybrid form as well.

Beyond the carmakers themselves, another way to play the future of hybrid cars is through the technology suppliers to the carmakers. Panasonic EV Energy (a 1966 joint venture between Toyota and Matsushita Electric Industrial), for instance, supplies NiMH batteries to both Toyota and Honda.

A more conservative, diversified play would be Matsushita Electric Industrial itself, the parent company of Panasonic EV Energy. Trading on the NYSE and with a market cap above $34 billion, Matsushita is a conglomerate of multiple brand names in audio, video, and communications equipment, home appliances, and industrial equipment. With revenues and net income rising steadily, and a PEG of only 0.5, the company is clearly undervalued. As the battery supplier to Toyota and Honda, Matsushita Electric will certainly ride the wave of hybrids as they flow onto the roads.

Putting It All Together:
A Portfolio for the Growing Oil Squeeze

As long as oil prices are rising at a moderate rate, a prudent investment plan would be to own a portfolio composed of 50 percent inflation hedges (precious metals, energy, and real estate), 30 percent Chindian stocks, and 20 percent deflation hedges (zero coupon bonds) as insurance.

In *The Oil Factor*, I proposed a strategy by which, if oil starts to rise sharply enough to run the risk of deflation (which we define as an 80 percent price rise in oil prices within the previous twelve months), investors would switch to 50 percent zero coupon bonds, and 20 percent inflation hedges. Once the year-over-year rise in oil prices falls to 20 percent or less, you would restore the prior pro-inflation weighting. By always keeping 20 percent of your savings in securities that provide insurance, you will gain protection from any sudden and unexpected inflation/deflation flip-flops.

This strategy still has merit, but only for those who are skilled at trading. The markets may be too volatile from now on for most investors to time successfully. However, the following portfolio should outperform using a simple buy-and-hold approach:

To position your portfolio to survive and thrive over the next few years, you could consider the following model portfolio:

Category	Securities	Typical weighting (oil rising or falling moderately)	Aggressive weighting (oil rising or falling rapidly)
Inflation hedges	**Precious metals** (gold, silver, and platinum stocks, funds, or bullion) e.g., Newmont, Barrick, Apex Silver, Impala Platinum, Tocqueville Gold Fund	25%	10%
	Energy (oil service companies, energy funds, and alternative energy stocks)	25%	10%
Chindia	(large-cap American companies expanding into China or India) e.g., 3M, Coca-Cola, Intel, Procter & Gamble, Texas Instruments	30%	30%
Deflation hedges	**Zero coupon bonds** e.g., American Century zero coupon funds	20%	50%

Wealth and Survival:
They're Really the Same Thing

As we said earlier, over the course of the next ten years, investors will either become much poorer or much wealthier than they are today. There is very little middle ground.

Doubtless, some people will follow our advice in the hope of becoming considerably wealthier. We fully expect they will succeed, and wish them great success in the endeavor.

However, in making these recommendations, we are mainly concerned with helping people avoid the groupthink trap that will make them poorer than they are today.

If our society does not begin taking steps to solve the energy crisis quickly, the most likely result is that today's complex society will become less complex in the future. We hope doomsday will not occur, but at the very least we expect there will be less of a social safety net in the future than there is today. This is why it is important for you to get on the right side of the trend now.

If you invest in securities vulnerable to inflation—our four investment pitfalls—and wind up poor, there may be no institution you can turn to that will make up for your mistakes; no inflation-indexed pension plan that delivers the full, promised benefits; no security firm or federal agency you can successfully sue for redress; no government with pockets deep enough to help the millions of elderly who need medical care, housing, and food.

Programs such as Social Security, Medicare, welfare, and others only became possible in the twentieth century because of a prosperity boom brought about by cheap oil. If we do not develop new, equally cheap, abundant energy sources in time, the government may lack the resources to address the needs of the poor and disadvantaged.

So we want you to get on the right side of the trends, to become wealthy, not just for wealth's sake, but for the survival of yourself and your family.

If it turns out we are completely wrong, and the world discovers new oil fields many times larger than those in the Middle East, that would still not derail the rapid growth of the Chindian sector. So we expect our model portfolio will produce good overall gains no matter what happens.

On the other hand, if we are largely correct, then our suggestions could help you avoid financial calamity and achieve far greater security and prosperity.

ography

[...]l Report on America's Energy Crisis."
Remarks b, [...] of Energy Spencer Abraham, U.S. Chamber of Commerce, National Energy Summit, March 19, 2001.

Asch, S. E. "Effects of Group Pressure upon the Modification and Distortion of Judgment." In J. Guetzkow, ed., *Groups, Leadership and Men.* Pittsburgh: Carnegie Press, 1951.

———. "Opinions and Social Pressure." *Scientific American* 193 (1955): 31–35.

Barberis, Nicholas, Andrei Shleifer, and Robert Vishny. "A Model of Investor Sentiment." *Journal of Financial Economics* 49 (1998): 307–43.

Benartzi, Shlomo, and Richard H. Thaler. "Myopic Loss Aversion and the Equity Premium Puzzle." *Quarterly Journal of Economics* 110, no. 1 (February 1995): 73–92.

Berryessa, Norman, and Eric Kirzner. *Global Investing the Templeton Way.* Homewood, IL: Dow Jones-Irwin, 1988.

Campbell, C. J., and J. H. Laherrere. "The End of Cheap Oil." *Scientific American,* March 1998: 78–83.

"China-Russia War Games Under Way, Aimed at US." *AsiaNews,* August 18, 2005.

Costantini, Valeria, and Francesco Gracceva. "Social Costs of Energy Disruptions." *Nota di Lavoro* 116 (September 2004).

Daly, Herman E. "Economics in a Full World." *Scientific American,* September 2005: 100–107.

Diamond, Jared. *Collapse: How Societies Choose to Fail or Succeed.* New York: Viking, 2005.

Doran, Michael Scott. "The Saudi Paradox." *Foreign Affairs,* January–February 2004: 35–51.

Engardio, Pete. "Crouching Tigers, Hidden Dragons: The Economic Momentum Isn't Unstoppable. China and India Face Huge Obstacles to Growth." *Business Week,* August 22, 2005, 60–61.

Evans, Harold, Gail Buckland, and David Lefer. *They Made America: From the Steam Engine to the Search Engine: Two Centuries of Innovators.* New York: Little, Brown, 2004.

Fuller, Buckminster. *Utopia or Oblivion: The Prospects for Mankind.* New York: Bantam, 1969.

Gilder, George. "Build It and They Will Come." *American Spectator,* November 1, 2000, 38.

Graham, Benjamin. *The Intelligent Investor.* 1949. New York: Harper-Collins, 2005.

Hagstrom, Robert G. *The Warren Buffett Way.* 2nd ed. Hoboken, NJ: John Wiley & Sons, 2005.

Haigh, Michael S., and John A. List. "Do Professional Traders Exhibit Myopic Loss Aversion? An Experimental Analysis." *Journal of Finance* 60, no. 1 (February 2005): 523–33.

Hirsch, Robert L., Roger H. Bezdek, and Robert M. Wendling. "Peaking Oil Production: Sooner Rather Than Later?" *Issues in Science and Technology,* April 1, 2005.

Hobbes, Thomas. *Leviathan.* 1651.

Hoffert, Martin I., et al. "Advanced Technology Paths to Global Climate Stability: Energy for a Greenhouse Planet." *Science,* November 1, 2002, 981–87.

"Images of Devastation, Anguish and Survival; New Orleans, August 30, 2005." *Newsweek,* September 12, 2005, 30.

International Energy Agency. "Resources to Reserves—Oil and Gas Technologies for the Energy Markets of the Future." Press release, September 22, 2005.

Ivanhoe, L. F. "Get Ready for Another Oil Shock." *The Futurist,* January 1, 1997.

Jacobson, Mark Z., and Gilbert M. Masters. "Exploiting Wind Versus Coal." *Science*, August 24, 2001, 1438.

———. "Response." Letters. *Science*, November 2, 2001, 1000–1003.

Jacobson, M. Z., W. G. Colella, and D. M. Golden. "Cleaning the Air and Improving Health with Hydrogen Fuel-Cell Vehicles." *Science*, June 24, 2005, 1901–5.

Janis, Irving L. *Groupthink: Psychological Studies of Policy Decisions and Fiascoes.* Rev. 2nd ed. Boston: Houghton Mifflin, 1982.

Kunstler, James Howard. *The Long Emergency: Surviving the Converging Catastrophes of the Twenty-First Century.* New York: Atlantic Monthly Press, 2005.

———. "The End of the Binge: The Exhaustion of Our Energy Supply May End Affluence as We Know It." *American Conservative*, September 12, 2005.

Langer, Thomas, and Martin Weber. "Myopic Prospect Theory vs. Myopic Loss Aversion: How General Is the Phenomenon?" *Journal of Economic Behavior and Organization* 56 (2005): 25–38.

Leeb, Stephen, and Donna Leeb. *Defying the Market: Profiting in the Turbulent Post-Technology Boom.* New York: McGraw-Hill, 1999.

———. *The Oil Factor: Protect Yourself—and Profit—from the Coming Energy Crisis.* New York: Warner Business Books, 2004.

Leeb, William. "Why Societies Fail: It's Not Just the Environment." *The Complete Investor*, September 2005: 12.

Lefevre, Edwin. *Reminiscences of a Stock Operator.* 1923. New York: John Wiley & Sons, 1993.

Lomborg, Bjorn, ed. *Global Crises, Global Solutions.* New York: Cambridge University Press, 2004.

Loomis, Carol. "Warren Buffett on the Stock Market." *Fortune*, December 6, 2001.

Lovins, Amory B. "More Profit with Less Carbon." *Scientific American*, September 2005: 74–83.

Maass, Peter. "The Breaking Point." *New York Times Magazine*, August 21, 2005, late edition, sec. 6, 30.

MacKenzie, James J. "Heading Off the Permanent Oil Crisis." *Issues in Science and Technology*, June 22, 1996.

Maurice, S. Charles, and C. W. Smithson. *The Doomsday Myth: 10,000 Years of Economic Crises*. Stanford, CA: Hoover Institution Press, 1984.

Milgram, Stanley. *Obedience to Authority: An Experimental View*. 1974. New York: Harper Perennial Modern Classics, 2004.

Moreira, Naila. "Growing Expectations: New Technology Could Turn Fuel into a Bumper Crop." *Science News*, October 1, 2005.

Morse, Edward L., and James Richard. "The Battle for Energy Dominance." *Foreign Affairs*, March–April 2002: 16–31.

Reich, Robert B. "The Paradox Explained." *American Prospect*, October 5, 2005, 48.

Rifkin, Jeremy. *The Hydrogen Economy: The Creation of the Worldwide Energy Web and the Redistribution of Power on Earth*. New York: Jeremy P. Tarcher/Penguin, 2002.

Rist, Curtis. "Why We'll Never Run Out of Oil." *Discover*, June 1999: 80–87.

Rokeach, Milton. *The Open and Closed Mind: Investigations into the Nature of Belief Systems and Personality Systems*. New York: Basic Books, 1960.

Ruddy, Christopher. "Sir John Templeton Reveals the Future of the Stock Market, Real Estate and Life." *Financial Intelligence Report*. Quoted at www.templetonpress.org/SirJohn/articles_details.asp#5e.

Ryan, Colleen. "Oil Basin Spat a Trough in Ties." *Australian Financial Review*, September 27, 2005.

Service, Robert F. "Is It Time to Shoot for the Sun?" *Science*, July 22, 2005.

Shields, Gerard. "House Passes Energy Bill Measure with $520 Million for La. Goes to Senate." *Baton Rouge Advocate*, July 29, 2005.

Shermer, Michael. "Why ET Hasn't Called." Skeptic. *Scientific American*, August 2002: 33.

Simmons, Matthew R. *Twilight in the Desert: The Coming Saudi Oil Shock and the World Economy*. Hoboken, NJ: John Wiley & Sons, 2005.

Soros, George. *The Alchemy of Finance: Reading the Mind of the Market*. New York: John Wiley & Sons, 1987, 1994.

"Special Report: Intelligence Failures—The Weapons That Weren't." *Economist*, July 15, 2004, 24.

Srobaugh, Robert, and Daniel Yergin. "Energy: An Emergency Telescoped." *Foreign Affairs* 58, no. 3 (1979).

Tainter, Joseph A. *The Collapse of Complex Societies. New Studies in Archaeology*. Cambridge, UK: Cambridge University Press, 1988.

Thaler, Richard H. "The End of Behavioral Finance." *Financial Analysts Journal* 55, no. 6 (1999): 12–17.

Urstadt, Bryant. "The Get-Ready Men: The Cheap Oil Will End One Day. What About Civilization?" Reviews. *Technology Review*, October 2005: 72–74.

Vaux, Gregson. "The Peak in U.S. Coal Production: LNG Import Issues Key." *From the Wilderness*, May 27, 2004. http://www.fromthewilderness.com/free/ww3/052504_coal_peak.html.

Index

Page numbers of charts and tables appear in italics.

About the Authors

STEPHEN LEEB edits the prestigious newsletter *The Complete Investor*. Renowned for consistently finishing among the leaders in the annual stock-picking contests of the *Wall Street Journal* and *Forbes*, he is the author of five previous books and holds a BA in economics, an MS in mathematics, and a PhD in psychology.

GLEN STRATHY is a freelance financial writer who writes from a secluded lake in Ontario, Canada. He holds an MA in English, a BA in English and Drama, and a BEd.